NORTH AMERICAN FRESHWATER FISHING

NORTH AMERICAN FRESHWATER FISHING

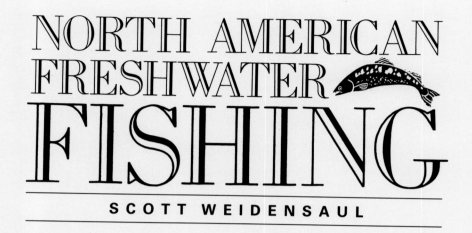

SCOTT WEIDENSAUL

GALLERY BOOKS

An Imprint of W. H. Smith Publishers Inc.

112 Madison Avenue
New York City 10016

A QUINTET BOOK

Produced for
GALLERY BOOKS
An imprint of W. H. Smith Publishers Inc.
112 Madison Avenue
New York, New York 10016

ISBN 0-8317-6433-3

This book was designed and produced by
Quintet Publishing Limited
6 Blundell Street
London N7 9BH

Creative Director: Peter Bridgewater
Art Director: Ian Hunt
Designer: Jonathan Roberts
Project Editor: Judith Simons

Typeset in Great Britain by
Central Southern Typesetters, Eastbourne
Manufactured in Hong Kong by
Regent Publishing Services Limited
Printed in Hong Kong by
Leefung-Asco Printers Limited

CONTENTS

Chapter One

GETTING STARTED

In a very real sense, fishing is a lot of different sports lumped together under one name. How else, then, to describe an activity that can range from tossing a feather-weight fly to a wild mountain trout, using sophisticated electronic gear and motorized downriggers to track salmon deep in the Great Lakes, fishing with stinkbait for giant catfish, or using foot-long suckers to lure trophy muskellunge?

Each kind of fishing has its own techniques, strategies and equipment requirements. So the first thing a beginner must decide is: What kind of fishing will I be doing?

Geography will determine part of the answer, because anglers generally fish for what's closest to home. If you live in the mountainous Northeast or New England, that probably means trout, smallmouth bass and pike. On the other hand, a fisherman in the South can expect to find largemouth bass, crappie and catfish close to home, but few coldwater species. In the Rockies, trout and mountain whitefish will be the most abundant quarry.

Personal preferences come into play as well. To some people, the idea of catching small native trout is a waste of time, while others abhor the idea of sitting by a sluggish river waiting for a carp or catfish to nibble the bait.

Perhaps the best place to start is with the basics of the three major kinds of fishing tackle – spinning, bait-casting and fly-fishing. The techniques used in casting each variety will be covered in the next chapter, *Basic Fishing Skills*.

S p i n - f i s h i n g

One of the handiest innovations of 20th-century angling was the invention of the open-face spinning reel just after World War II. With it, even an amateur can quickly master the skills needed to effortlessly toss off long, smooth casts, using a variety of lures and lines. Spinning is probably the best overall method of fishing – and the most widely used.

A spinning reel has an open line receptacle that faces forward, toward the rod tip. A hundred or more yards of line are wound onto an open spool, held in place by a spring-loaded wire bail. When the angler is ready to cast, he hooks the line with his index finger, then flips back the bail, freeing the line. As he casts, he releases his finger, and the weight of the lure carries line off the reel.

Once the cast is complete, the bail can be flipped back by hand, or will do so automatically when the reel handle is turned. Gears inside the reel multiply each revolution of the handle, so the line can be quickly retrieved. During the retrieve, the bail revolves around the spool, automatically winding the line back on.

All good spinning rods have a drag adjustment somewhere on the reel. Drag is the amount of tension put on the line when the bail is closed. With light drag, a fish can peel line off the reel with little resistance, but by tightening the drag, an angler can make the fish

OPPOSITE *An old square-tailed brook trout slaps the water in a cartwheeling leap.*

ABOVE *Heavy level-wind reels are a good choice for fishing downriggers in deep water for fish like this Great Lakes salmon.*

work harder, thus tiring itself more quickly. Tight drag poses a danger, however, because any sudden or extreme pressure can break the line. On most models the drag is a dial set in the front center of the reel, although on some spinning rods the drag control is at the back or underside of the reel.

Spin-fishing rods average from 5 to 8 feet long, with a smooth grip that extends several inches behind the reel seat. The line guides on a spinning rod are fairly large near the base, because during the cast the line peels off the reel in a fairly open spiral.

A variation of the spinning reel is the closed-face (or spin-cast) reel, a push-button affair that is very easy to use – one of the reasons it has traditionally been considered a child's reel. Spin-cast outfits won't cast as far as open-face reels because the line, as it spins off the spool, must pass through a hole in the spool cover that causes drag and slows it down. Instead of a bail that is opened for each cast, the closed-face reel has a large push-button that, when released, frees the line. Most spin-cast reels are designed for use on a bait-casting rod that has a protruding index finger grip.

Few serious spinning fishermen use spin-cast outfits, preferring an open-face reel instead.

■ WHAT SIZE OUTFIT? ■

Spinning gear comes in four weights: heavy, medium, light and ultra-light. What weight you use depends on what you're fishing for, and how. In each case, matching the proper rod action, reel capability, line and lure size is essential if you want to get the most out of your gear.

■ **HEAVY ACTION** spinning outfits are meant to handle the toughest fish and strongest lines – fish like the largest carp and catfish, muskies and big salmon. The rods are stout, with a lot of backbone, and the reels have rugged drags. Line size: 20 pound and up.

■ **MEDIUM ACTION** outfits can handle big fish, too, but the angler must exercise greater care during the fight, because the line and rod cannot take as much punishment. Medium gear is best for large bass, catfish, trout, pike, walleye and other species. Line size: 8-17 pounds. Some rods, marketed as "medium-heavy," are the best choice for the upper range of lines.

■ **LIGHT GEAR** is terrific for getting the most out of a fish. Heavier lines dampen the battle and telegraph little of the lunges and runs a fish makes, but lightweight tackle allows the angler to experience all the thrill. Light outfits work best when matched with thinner lines, in the 4 to 8 pound range.

■ **ON ULTRALIGHT TACKLE,** a 12-inch smallmouth feels like a whale – the biggest reason for the growing popularity of super-lightweight rods, reels and lines. The reel is loaded with 2- or 4-pound test line, and should have a drag that can be finely set. Ultralight outfits are easy to cast all day with little fatigue, and are most efficient when coupled with small, light lures. This is the perfect choice for panfish, stream trout and bass.

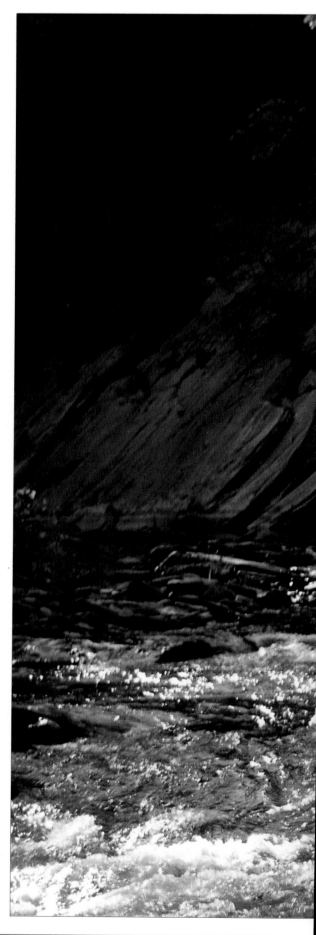

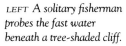

LEFT A solitary fisherman probes the fast water beneath a tree-shaded cliff.

B a i t - c a s t i n g

The name is misleading, because bait-casting outfits (or just "casting" in some circles) are most effective for dropping lures with pinpoint accuracy.

In years past, bait-casting reels had a richly deserved reputation for difficult use – a problem then inherent in the design of the reel. The spool is at right angles to the rod, unlike the forward-facing spool of a spinning rod. The angler must use his thumb to control the line during the cast, and even more important, must thumb down on the spool just as the lure splashes down. Otherwise, the spool keeps spinning, causing a tangled backlash.

RIGHT *Bait-cast reels are popular among bass fishermen because they provide pin-point accuracy when casting a wide variety of lures.*

OPPOSITE *A bait-cast outfit (top) is held with the reel uppermost, using the thumb to apply pressure to the line. A spinning reel, on the other hand, hangs below the rod, and the index finger is used to control the line (bottom).*

Thankfully, most modern bait-casting reels now have anti-backlash devices, and are much easier to use. Even so, a bait-casting outfit requires more skill to use than a spinning outfit, and can be frustrating for the beginner.

Bait-casting reels require a specialized rod – usually shorter than spinning rods, with a finger grip below the reel seat.

C h o o s i n g   t h e
r i g h t   l i n e

Modern technology has revolutionized fishing in many ways, some apparent and some not. Monofilament line is a good example, as chemical companies compete to promote their brands by increasing their strength, decreasing diameter and eliminating old problems like "memory," monofilament's unfortunate tendency to stay coiled even

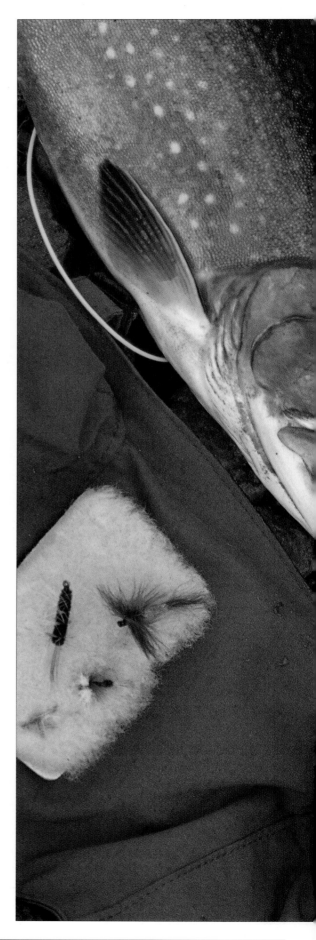

after it is off the reel. Such advances are of genuine benefit, but, frankly, differences between the major brands are small, and any one will serve well.

More important than brand selection is the choice of the proper line size. Mono is manufactured in varying *pound-tests*, depending on its normal breaking strength. Thus, 12-pound-test line can stand more pressure than 2-pound-test, although both can probably take more strain than their rated test strength. Obviously, larger fish usually call for heavier line, although experienced fishermen routinely catch enormous fish on light line. The secret is in carefully playing the fish on a light drag setting, usually during a prolonged fight.

Most monofilament is transparent, but it is generally accepted that fish can see even lightweight line. Nevertheless, the number of strikes usually increases when you use lighter test line, because it is not as obtrusive as heavier weights, and will not scare off as many fish.

Match your line not just to the fish you are seeking, but the action of your outfit. As previously mentioned, rods and reels work best when coupled with the right size line; the line rating is usually marked on the reel and rod themselves. Line size is also critical to lure performance and casting; a line that is too heavy for the lure reduces casting distance and interferes with lure action.

F l y - f i s h i n g

There are few more graceful sights in fishing than an experienced fly-fisherman effortlessly throwing 40 or 50 feet of line, then dropping a dry fly in just the right spot to elicit a strike. Fly-fishing has a mystique all its own, and a reputation as the hardest technique to learn – a reputation that is baseless if the beginner selects the proper gear and is willing to practice with it.

In spin-fishing and bait-casting, the weight of the lure carries the thin line on behind during the cast. In fly-fishing, the roles are reversed – the rather heavy fly line provides the mass needed to send an almost weightless fly on its way. To keep that line moving through the air requires a special kind of rod, and a completely different casting technique.

▌ FLY RODS ▌

Fly rods are long, averaging 7 or 8 feet, and more supple than spinning or bait-casting rods. The reel is of simple design – a level-wind spool, usually with a 1-to-1 retrieve ratio, meaning that the spool turns once for each turn of the handle, unlike the multiplying gears in spinning reels. A fly-fisherman does not play the fish off the reel, but rather uses finger tension on the line itself to control the action. Even reels designed for big fish, and equipped with drag systems, usually also are made to be "palmed," applying hand pressure to the spool edge to slow a fish down.

Fly outfits, like spinning sets, come in various weights, from 1- or 2-weights (ultralight), through 5-weight and 6-weight rods, the norm

for trout fishing. Fly-rodding for bass, which requires bulky streamers and hairbugs, calls for an 8-weight outfit, while salmon, steelhead and pike fishermen usually prefer a 9- or 10-weight rod. The rod and line weights *must* match, or the outfit will be impossible to cast well. This is perhaps the most common mistake made by neophyte fly-rodders, and one that accounts for much of fly-fishing's blemished reputation as a difficult sport to learn.

▮ FLY LINES AND LEADERS ▮

Fly line comes in floating, sinking and sinking-tip designs, each for a particular use: floating for dry flies or shallow streams, sinking and sinking-tips for deeper water with wet flies and streamers. The line may be level, that is, one diameter its entire length, or tapered at each end. Such double-tapered lines are somewhat more expensive, but are by far the easiest to cast, and are universally recommended. During the cast, the rod flexes, throwing a loop into the line. A taper transmits this energy more efficiently down the length of line, making it roll over properly. In a level line the energy transfer is dampened, and the line may simply fall in a heap.

Fly line is obviously too bulky to tie a fly to, so the final piece of fly-fishing gear is the leader, an 8- or 9-foot length of monofilament. It is essential that the leader, too, be tapered; one can either purchase a knotless tapered leader, or make one from progressively thinner weights of standard monofilament. The thinnest end of the leader is known as the tippet, and must be matched to the size fly being used: a 1-pound tippet, for example, is perfect for a tiny dry fly, but will snap off a heavy, weighted nymph during the cast. By the same token, a heavy 6-pound tippet would sink a dry fly, but is ideal for use with a big streamer.

ARTIFICIALS VERSUS BAIT

Lures or bait? Some anglers swear by live bait, insisting that the biggest fish fall to their natural prey. Others look down their noses at the real thing, preferring the challenge of fooling a fish with an artificial lure.

In truth, each has its uses, and both are effective in the hands of an experienced angler. The key is in knowing when to use what.

LEFT A medium-weight fly-fishing outfit and a Muddler minnow brought this beautiful brook trout to net.

L u r e s

Ever since the ancient Greeks first tied a hank of red wool to a hook, or the first Indian dangled a carved, wooden minnow through the ice to tempt a pike within spear range, fishermen have used artificial lures. Today, the vast array of patterns is bewildering, filling entire

ABOVE *Spinners come in a wide range of colors and sizes, but all share the same basic design – a central shaft around which a flashy blade revolves.*

catalogs. But most are simply variations on a few, basic designs, each for a different style of fishing. Oddly, although highly realistic lures work well, so do those that imitate absolutely nothing in nature. Fish react to more than just color and form – sound, movement and behavior all play at least as important a role in sparking a strike.

JIGS

Jigs have a single hook that rides point-up, with a lead head for weight, a colored body and tail originally made of chenille and marabou feather. The introduction of plastic-bodied models in the 1970s revolutionized jig fishing, however. Today, the most popular sort, like the Mister Twister and related brands, have a soft plastic body and a long, curled tail that corkscrews through the water during the retrieve. Fished in various colors, and in sizes from 1/64th of an ounce to half an ounce, they will catch virtually any freshwater fish. Jigs can be either cast out and retrieved, or fished vertically like a yo-yo – "jigging," in other words.

PLASTIC WORMS

Once plastic worms were molded and colored to look just like the real thing, but no more. Most now feature a curled tail for better action, and come in a rainbow of colors, with black, purples, blues and maroon the most popular. Used most often for bass, worms are also good for pickerel, pike and occasionally large trout and walleye. Rig a worm by threading the eye of a single hook through the nose of the worm, then burying the barb of the hook farther back in the worm's body. The result should have the curved hook shank protruding downward like the keel of a boat. A slip sinker on the line in front of the worm will take the lure to the bottom, where it is fished with a slow, twitching retrieve. Because the hook point is buried in the worm, this rig is almost completely weedless.

SPINNERS

Spinners are highly effective for game fish that prey on minnows, because the polished metal blade, spinning through the water, creates the effect of small fish trying to flee. Silver and gold are the most widely used colors, although black, orange and a host of fluorescent hues can be deadly in certain conditions. Some spinners have a skirt of squirrel fur that hides the treble hooks. Spinners can be retrieved at a steady pace, but varying the rate of retrieve – even stopping it momentarily and letting the lure flutter down through the water – can spark a savage strike.

SPINNERBAITS

Spinnerbaits are an impressionistic marriage between spinners and lead jigs, and are a fairly recent addition to the tacklebox. Created for use on southern largemouth bass, they have proven effective as well for smallmouth, pike, muskie and other species. Most feature one or two metal spinner blades, connected by a bent wire to a lead jig with a fringed rubber skirt that pulsates through the water. Essentially weedless, they can be fished in thick cover, and at speeds from a dead crawl to a rapid, wake-churning pace.

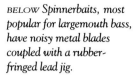

BELOW Spinnerbaits, most popular for largemouth bass, have noisy metal blades coupled with a rubber-fringed lead jig.

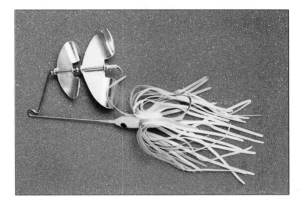

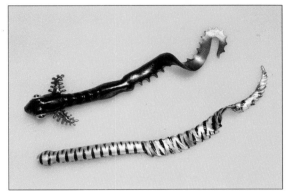

ABOVE Plastic "worms" do not always even remotely resemble the real thing; the lure at top, for instance, has eyes and external gills to mimic an aquatic salamander.

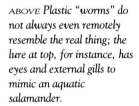

LEFT Jigs are among the most effective lures available, and – depending on the size used – can catch everything from muskies to sunfish.

RIGHT *Many diving plugs, like these crankbaits, sport fluorescent colors, which show up better in deep water where sunlight is muted.*

ABOVE *Crankbaits, like this shad imitation, have large, plastic lips that force them to dive deep when retrieved.*

OPPOSITE LEFT *Floater/diver minnows are effective plugs for many game fish, which react to the "crippled minnow" action imparted by the plug's long shape and plastic lip.*

OPPOSITE RIGHT *The basic fly patterns: from left, a downwing caddis dry, a marabou streamer, a nymph, a wet fly and a classic March Brown dry fly.*

▌ SPOONS ▌

Long prized for their deadliness on pike, muskie, salmon and trout, spoons or wobblers are enjoying increasing use among bass and pan-fish anglers as well. The general shape is roughly that of a table spoon with the handle cut off, with a treble hook trailing from the end. Most spoons wobble and flutter as they move through the water. Red-and-white is the traditional North Country combination, but metallic and fluorescent colors are the best choices for salmon.

▌ PLUGS ▌

There are, by far, more varieties of plugs than any other group of lures.
■ **FLOATING PLUGS** include such realistic bait-fish imitations as the Rapala and Rebel minnows – long and slim, painted in silver, blue, gold or another natural color. At rest, balsa wood or plastic lures float, but when they are retrieved, a down-turned plastic lip forces them to dive and imparts a side-to-side wobble. They are best fished in short pulls, twitched for a moment and then allowed to float back to the top, mimicking the movements of a crippled minnow.

Other floating plugs do not imitate fish. The classic Jitterbug, for

example, is a topwater plug with a cylindrical body and curved metal faceplate that makes the lure wiggle wildly, gurgling across the surface. The Hula Popper, another old favorite, has a concave face. Brought in with short pulls, it splashes with each spurt – the kind of noise that sounds to fish like injured prey. Many floating plugs have blades or propellers for similar noisemaking.

■ **FLOATER/DIVER PLUGS,** among them the crankbaits, are made to dive almost straight down and run in deep water, but to float to the top as soon as the retrieve is stopped.

■ **SINKING PLUGS** are built to run shallow or deep, and often sink at a predetermined rate, allowing the angler to "count down" to the desired depth. Most are patterned after forage fish like shiners or shad, tadpoles or crayfish. Many contain metal pellets that rattle during the retrieve, sending out vibrations that fish can sense even after dark, or in muddy water.

All these lures are equally effective fished with spinning or bait-casting gear, but are far too heavy to use with a fly-fishing outfit. For that, one needs lightweight flies, tied of feathers, fur and synthetic materials. The hook sizes are numbered in reverse order; thus a size 28 fly is tiny, while a size 6 is much larger.

▌ DRY FLIES ▌

Dry flies, simply put, are those that float on the surface and imitate an insect (other surface flies, like bass bugs, are not usually considered dry flies.) The classic dry is one that mimics a mayfly, a common aquatic insect. Long fibers from rooster hackles match the long tails of the natural, and provide balance to the fly. The fur body matches the insect's general color, and hackle feathers, wound around the hook to form a circular ruff, keep the fly above the surface film of the water. Other dries imitate the adult stages of caddisflies and stoneflies, two common stream insects that crawl to the surface of the water, shed their nymphal skin and unfurl wings. Trout, bass and other fish go into feeding frenzies during such hatches, and produce some of the best fly-fishing around.

Still other dry flies imitate terrestrial bugs like grasshoppers, beetles

ABOVE An angler selects a
wet fly from a well-stocked
flybox – a prerequisite for
successful fly-fishing.

RIGHT Prepared salmon
eggs are a popular bait
for trout, salmon and
steelhead. Short-shanked
hooks work best when
fishing them.

and ants, which frequently fall into the water during warm weather. In the West, grasshoppers are a particularly important trout food, and there are dozens of slightly different patterns to match them.

▌ WET FLIES ▌

Wet flies are fished under the surface, and are meant to suggest the larval forms of aquatic insects. Most are drab shades of brown or gray, but a few patterns, like the Royal Coachman or the red-and-white Parmachene Belle, are brightly colored attractors, the fly-fishing equivalent of a fluorescent plug.

▪ **NYMPHS** are a special class of wet fly (indeed, many fly-fishermen consider them completely separate.) They accurately imitate mayfly, caddis and stonefly larvae, and usually have a flattened body and a dark wingcase over the top of the abdomen, just as the naturals have.

▌ STREAMERS ▌

Streamers are large flies that imitate fish. They tend to be flashier and more impressionistic than dries or wets, dressed with bucktail (dyed or natural white,) feathers and tinsel. Fished in quick, erratic spurts, they are known as "big fish flies" because so many trophy fish eat nothing but minnows. Streamers work well in small sizes for panfish, while those used for pike may be 6 or 8 inches long.

L i v e   b a i t

Live bait can be a problem, without a doubt. It can be expensive to buy, time-consuming to catch and hard to keep alive until it's needed. But there are times when only the real thing seems to work. Here's a rundown of the most important kinds of bait, how to get them, keep them and use them.

▌ EARTHWORMS ▌

Earthworms are probably the most widely used live bait in North America. They range from small garden worms to foot-long nightcrawlers, and their squirming action and aroma account for their appeal to fish. Worms are also the easiest bait to get – a few shovelsful of soil almost anywhere will likely turn up a few. The best worm habitat is in rich, moist soil – gardens, flowerbeds, damp woodlands and lawns. In dry weather, worms retreat deep into the ground, but prolonged soaking from a lawn sprinkler can bring them to the top.

Nightcrawlers are large worms that crawl partly out of their holes on damp, mild nights. Catch them by creeping along softly, grabbing the worms just where they enter the ground. Slow, steady pressure will ease the nightcrawler out of its hole, but too much pull will snap it off. Nightcrawlers are light-shy, and react with amazing speed if a strong beam hits them. Use a dim flashlight, or partially mask the beam with your fingers.

Commercial worm bedding (actually finely pulped paper,) grass clippings and moist straw work well as a storage medium for worms,

BELOW *A stonefly nymph with a wet fly (right) and two nymph patterns that imitate it.*

© JOE REYNOLDS

ABOVE *After spending a year as an aquatic nymph, the mayfly is transformed into a delicate, winged adult that trout find irresistible as food. Classic dry fly patterns imitate this phase of the insect's life.*

but plain dirt is actually a bad choice because it compacts too much; a 50-50 blend of dirt and grass is much better. Worms feed on decaying vegetation in the soil, so make sure the bedding has lots of organic matter. Keep the worms damp (but not wet) and somewhere cool. Even a short period of direct sun and heat kills worms very quickly, and a dead worm is worse than useless as bait.

Worms can be fished in many ways – simply threaded on a hook, used to tip a jig or spinner, partially inflated with air from a syringe, on the bottom of or suspended from a bobber, among other methods. They are good bait for almost any fish – even pike and muskies have been known to fall for a gob of nightcrawlers.

▌ BAIT FISH ▌

Bait fish include minnows, shiners, chubs, sunfish, suckers and small catfish. The choice depends on the conditions and the quarry – stream-dwelling trout more readily accept minnows, while smallmouth bass in rivers like small catfish such as madtoms.

Small bait fish can be taken in traps or nets. Minnow traps are usually mesh cylinders, with a small opening at each end. Baited with meal or fish scraps and suspended where minnows congregate, they do their job with little or no attention. Nets require more work, but often with better results. In streams, 4-by-4-foot seines work best; attach them at either side to poles, and while one person holds the net in the current, another wades downstream toward it, rolling over rocks and herding the minnows in (stirring up the mud to hide the net will greatly increase your catch.) In lakes, frame nets and casting nets are better, because they can be used from a boat.

Before taking bait fish, check the regulations in your state or province; some techniques that are legal in one may be prohibited in another, and many states have limits on how many fish can be taken at one time. Also, some species may be off-limits for use as bait. For example, most states have banned the use of goldfish because escapees can be terrible pests.

Stream minnows must be kept in cool, running water if they are to survive. Large quantities are best housed in wooded boxes with mesh sides and bottom, anchored in the creek. Because the mesh will keep out food, the minnows must be fed regularly. While fishing, commercial minnow buckets of metal or plastic are the best bet, with frequent water changes a must. Warmwater species, like chubs and catfish, can tolerate higher water temperatures and less dissolved oxygen, but they, too, do best in screened boxes kept in flowing water.

Bait fish can be fished alive, hooked lightly through the lips, back or tail, or dead with a commercial minnow rig. Live bait fish are most effective when fished with as little encumbrance as possible, so they move naturally. A plastic bobber and no weight is usually the preferred rig. For very large fish, like muskies, big pike and trophy bass, exceptionally large bait fish are needed – in the case of muskellunge, suckers a foot long are commonly used. Such bait fish are usually caught with hook and line.

OPPOSITE A seine net provides an easy way of catching minnows, crayfish, hellgrammites and other aquatic bait.

ABOVE Use a dim light and careful movements to catch nightcrawlers, which surface on warm, damp evenings.

RIGHT The maw of a largemouth bass can easily engulf fish, frogs – and well-placed lures.

BELOW RIGHT Small frogs are top bait for bass, pike and other large game fish.

OTHER BAITS

Not every bait is live. Catfish anglers swear by stinkbaits, awful concoctions of ripe chicken guts, blood and other smelly ingredients that attract catfish. Carp fishermen often use doughballs, flavored with gelatin mix. Corn kernels, cheese and even tiny marshmallows will catch stocked trout, which apparently mistake the bait for the pelletized food they were fed in the hatchery – hardly a compliment to the instincts of stocked fish.

▌ MEALWORMS AND GRUBS ▌

Mealworms and grubs are good bait for panfish and trout. Most fishermen simply buy mealworms (also known as mealies,) but they are easy to raise in large quantities. Mealworms are not worms at all, but are the larvae of *Tenebrio* beetles, a major pest in stored grains. Place the mealworms in deep plastic trays (plastic shoeboxes are perfect,) with a supply of grain and a half-potato for moisture, and let them breed. This is definitely a garage project, because the odor of a mealworm colony is not pleasant.

In some areas, maggots and other grubs are favorite panfish bait. Because of their food habits, they are obviously best purchased, rather than raised. Fish mealworms and grubs on small, light hooks, with a minimum of weight.

▌ GRASSHOPPERS AND CRICKETS ▌

Grasshoppers and crickets are an excellent summertime bait for trout, bass and panfish. Search through tall grass early in the morning, when the cool air has the grasshoppers in a state of dormancy. They do not keep well for more than a day or so, and are best if collected fresh each morning. Crickets, which can also be bought through pet and bait shops, fare better in captivity. To keep your whole supply of grasshoppers and crickets from jumping out of the bait jar every time the lid is opened, try this trick – put a wad of nylon stocking in the bottom of the jar. The insects' hooked feet snag in the fine mesh, and they can be removed one at a time.

Fish crickets and grasshoppers on the surface or just below it. Slip a fine-wired hook under the thorax, or collar, so the bug remains uninjured and lively. A clear plastic casting bobber will help get the bait out farther with spinning tackle.

▌ FROGS AND SALAMANDERS ▌

Frogs and salamanders (often erroneously called "lizards") are good bass, pike and pickerel bait. Small frogs work best; look for them along grassy stream banks and marshy areas. If legal in your area, they can also be caught at night with a flashlight. Aquatic salamanders like mudpuppies can be caught with a minnow net, or by carefully lifting flat rocks and grabbing them as they flee.

As with minnows, hook the animal lightly through the lips or a leg. Many fishermen, to keep their bait lively and to avoid injuring it, will use frog harnesses that hold the hook in place with rubber bands.

▌ HELLGRAMMITES AND CRAYFISH ▌

Hellgrammites and crayfish are unmatched as smallmouth bass bait. The hellgrammite, the aquatic larvae of the dobsonfly, is a worm-like bug with a pair of sharp, powerful jaws, commonly found beneath rocks in rivers and large streams. Use a seine while rolling rocks to catch them, then keep them in a minnow bucket – hellgrammites require much the same care as minnows.

Crayfish will catch more than just smallmouths. Most game fish will

BELOW Crayfish comprise a large part of the diet of many game fish, making them a logical choice as bait.

ABOVE Early morning is the best time to collect fast-moving grasshoppers, when they are still chilled from the cool night air.

eat freshly molted crayfish, known as soft-shells, which are flabby and pale. Like hellgrammites, crayfish are easiest to catch with a minnow seine in shallow water, kicking over rocks to chase them into the net. Many people prefer to catch soft-shells by hand, however, slowly lifting rocks, poised to grab if there's one underneath.

Other gear

Besides lures, a well-stocked tacklebox contains a few other essentials.

■ **LEAD SINKERS** help get the lure or bait down to the proper level, and keep it there. For general use, a pack of split-shot is best; the most versatile are those with lobes that can be pinched to open the shot when it must be removed. For fishing in strong current, heavier weights are needed, although a common mistake is using too much lead – fish strike more freely at bait with natural action, and a lead sinker cancels that action.

■ **BOBBERS,** or floats, have two functions: to keep the bait suspended at a certain level, and to signal the strike, and are used almost exclusively with bait. The most common type is the classic round, red-and-white bobber, with spring-loaded hooks in the stem and on the bottom to secure the line. Pencil floats, tapered pieces of wood or plastic, have more sensitivity than standard round bobbers.

■ **SWIVELS** and snap-swivels prevent rotating lures, like spinners, from twisting the line and causing tangles. The snap also provides an easy way to change lures without retying knots each time. Silver and gold are traditional colors, but plain black is gaining popularity on the assumption that it does not scare fish. A word of caution on using snap swivels with lures: in many cases the extra weight of the swivel reduces the lure's built-in action, and thus its effectiveness.

■ Bait-fishermen have a wide variety of **HOOKS** from which to choose, ranging from barb-shanked worm hooks to double-pointed minnow hooks, and cricket hooks with a safety pin assembly for securing the insect. As a rule of thumb, use the smallest hook possible, hiding most of it in the bait whenever possible to avoid spooking the fish.

■ **NETS** are not necessary for smaller fish, which can be landed as easily by hand. For bigger fish, an aluminum net with a nylon mesh bag will last for years without rusting or rotting. To keep your catch alive and fresh while fishing, use a **STRINGER** or wire fish basket; metal stringers are most popular, but new models made of tough nylon work just as well, and do not rattle or clank. Fish baskets are cumbersome except for dock or boat fishing.

■ A pair of **NEEDLE-NOSED PLIERS** are invaluable for unhooking fish, especially those like pike or walleye with sharp teeth. Fly-fishermen often prefer **HEMOSTATS** or curved surgical clamps, which have more delicacy than pliers for removing small flies. A pair of **NAIL CLIPPERS** works better than teeth for snipping off lures and trimming the tag ends of knots.

■ **THE TACKLEBOX** itself can be as large or small as personal preference (and the size of your lure collection) dictates. Choose one with adjustable compartments that can be enlarged for big lures. Today, almost all tackleboxes are made of high-strength plastic, so problems with rusting are a thing of the past.

■ **FISHING VESTS** are of interest to fly-fishermen, spin-fishermen and others who wade, and obviously can't tote a heavy tacklebox along with them. Some deluxe vests offer as many as 35 or 40 pockets, using virtually all available space. Not surprisingly, the amount of gear and gadgets usually expands to fill those pockets – an inescapable rule of fishing physics.

■ **POLARIZED SUNGLASSES** are a must for fishermen, both to prevent eyestrain from bright, reflected light, and to make it easier to see the fish. Polarized glasses greatly reduce glare and reflections so an angler can see what's going on beneath the surface – not just what's mirrored on top.

■ **INSECT REPELLENT** is essential in many areas, but be careful – what's repellent to bugs also turns off fish. Keep the repellent out of the tacklebox, and make sure it doesn't get on the line or lures. For that reason, liquid repellents are usually better than aerosol cans, which create an enveloping fog. Be especially careful to keep the repellent off your hands, and wash well after spraying, before handling your gear.

■ Still the subject of some controversy are **FISHING SCENTS**, which when sprayed on lures are said to attract fish; others come in solid form, to be molded on the hook, slipped into compartments in special lures or rubbed on from a stick. Some anglers swear by scents, others have seen little difference when using them. Certainly they do no harm, and may tip the scales in your favor on a slow day. Most scents come in different formulas for specific species, or simply imitate the aroma of particular baits.

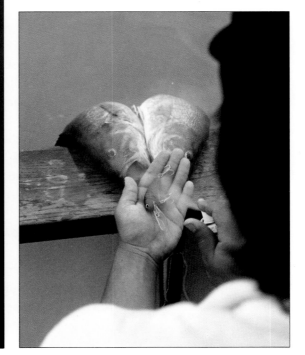

FAR LEFT A net is invaluable for landing fish. Match the net size to the quarry, because trying to land a fish in a skimpy net is a recipe for disaster.

LEFT Many anglers swear by the use of artificial scents, sprayed on lures to make them more attractive to fish. This scented crankbait has already accounted for two nice smallmouth bass.

Extending your reach

BELOW The pinnacle of
fishing technology, modern
bass boats are equipped with
everything from depthfinders
to dissolved oxygen meters.

ABOVE Rubberized chest
waders, like the pair at left,
can offer insulation for
coldwater fishing, but
stocking-foot waders, worn
with boot liners and wading
shoes, are much more
comfortable for most
angling.

Fish aren't always right along the shore – in fact, the best fishing is often in the deeper channels or off rocky points, in places not accessible to a land-based fisherman. In those situations, the answer is boots or boats.

For streams and rivers, boots will probably be adequate for the job. Rubber hip boots, which come to the middle of the thigh, are of limited value; the best fishing always seems to be *just* beyond their depth. A much better choice are chest waders, which extend the protection to armpit level.

Waders come in rubberized cloth, lightweight nylon or neoprene. Rubberized waders are able to stand hard use, but tend to crack during storage and are heavy and confining, hot in the sun and freezing cold in chilly water. Neoprene – the same material diving suits are made from – is more flexible, and its superior insulating abilities make it the best choice for cold-weather fishing; however, neoprene waders can be a mobile sauna in warm weather. Stockingfoot waders are extremely light, made of a thin layer of tough nylon with a sock-like foot that is slipped into a heavier wading shoe. They are inexpensive and comfortable to wear, and although they have virtually no insulation value, most can easily be worn over wool socks and heavy clothes for extra warmth.

If your wading will take you over slippery rocks, be certain whatever waders you buy have felt soles, which provide excellent traction on algae and scum. Plain boot soles – even those with deep tread – are dangerously slick on such surfaces. A belt around your waist on the outside of the waders is also a good idea to keep out water when you (inevitably) fall in.

A relatively new hybrid between boots and boats are the belly boats, really nothing more than a large inner tube enclosed in a nylon cover, with a fabric seat in the hole. Wearing waders, the fisherman sits in the seat, propelling himself with a pair of swimmer's foot fins. Belly boats are popular for bass and panfish, and for trout fishing in Western lakes.

Fishing boats run the gamut from canoes to cabin cruisers, with prices ranging from $100 to many thousands. Some bass boats sport enough electronic gear to guide a moon mission – fishfinders, depth finders, pH gauges, electric thermometers, even lure-selection computers.

It is safe to say, however, that the best overall fishing boat is a simple, flat-bottomed johnboat capable of carrying two or three people, and powered by a small outboard motor. A battery-powered trolling motor, which moves the boat with very little noise, is another handy piece of equipment. Such a boat is very stable, and while it is not designed for use on big lakes or whitewater, it is perfect for most lakes, ponds and rivers.

© JOE REYNOLDS

LEFT A canoe is the perfect craft for fishing quiet lakes and moving water, although its easy maneuverability is offset by a lack of room and stability.

ABOVE Caught from a cabin cruiser, a huge chinook salmon comes to the net amid an orderly tangle of rods, bent beneath the strain of downrigger weights. When the fish hits, the weight snaps free, allowing the fisherman to fight without encumbrance.

LEFT Belly boats provide easy access to lakes and ponds, without the expense or difficulty of towing a real boat.

Chapter Two

BASIC FISHING SKILLS

Choosing the right gear is half the battle in fishing. The other half is learning how to use it properly – the basic skills like knot-tying and casting – as well as learning to interpret the conditions to find fish, and how to react once the strike comes.

K n o t s

Spinning and bait-cast fishermen really need only one knot for their sport, while the fly-fisherman has more specialized requirements that call for several additional knots.

Monofilament can be slippery and difficult to handle, especially when one is trying to tie an unfamiliar knot. Old fly line or smooth twine makes a good practice cord, until you master the knot.

OPPOSITE Beneath the sagebrush hills of Colorado, a fly-fisherman works his way through a rich pool on the Eagle River.

▮ THE IMPROVED CLINCH KNOT ▮

The improved clinch knot is the most universally useful knot in fishing. Used for tying a lure or fly to the line, it is simple to learn, won't slip and retains much of the line's strength – an important consideration, because when mono is tied into a knot, it unavoidably loses some of its breaking power.

To tie the improved clinch knot, thread the line through the eye of the hook, then wrap the tag (or loose) end of the mono around the standing portion of the line six times. Pass the tag end through the loop that has formed above the hook eye, then back up through the second, higher loop. Pull gently taut. If the knot is properly tied, it should slide down to form a neat series of loops, with the tag end protruding from the top; clip it off close to the knot with nail clippers.

The improved clinch can be used to tie line to bare hooks, lures, flies, swivels – in fact, to almost anything except another piece of line.

▮ THE BLOOD KNOT ▮

To make a line-to-line attachment, such as for a knotted leader for fly-fishing, use the blood knot, or barrel knot.

Form an X with the two ends of monofilament, allowing several inches of excess on each. Take one end and wrap it four times round the other piece of monofilament, then bend it back, slipping the end through the gap at the beginning of the wraps, where the X forms. Do the same with the other piece of mono, slipping it through the gap from the opposite direction. Hold the tag ends in your teeth without pulling them, and tighten the knot by pulling on the two standing pieces. The knot should slip together, forming a neat series of wraps. Trim the tag ends closely, or leave one hanging free to serve as the leader for a dropper fly.

▮ SURGEON'S LOOP AND LOOP-TO-LOOP CONNECTION ▮

A handy leader connection is to use two surgeon's loops, which are easy to tie but should not be used with large fish, as they do not have

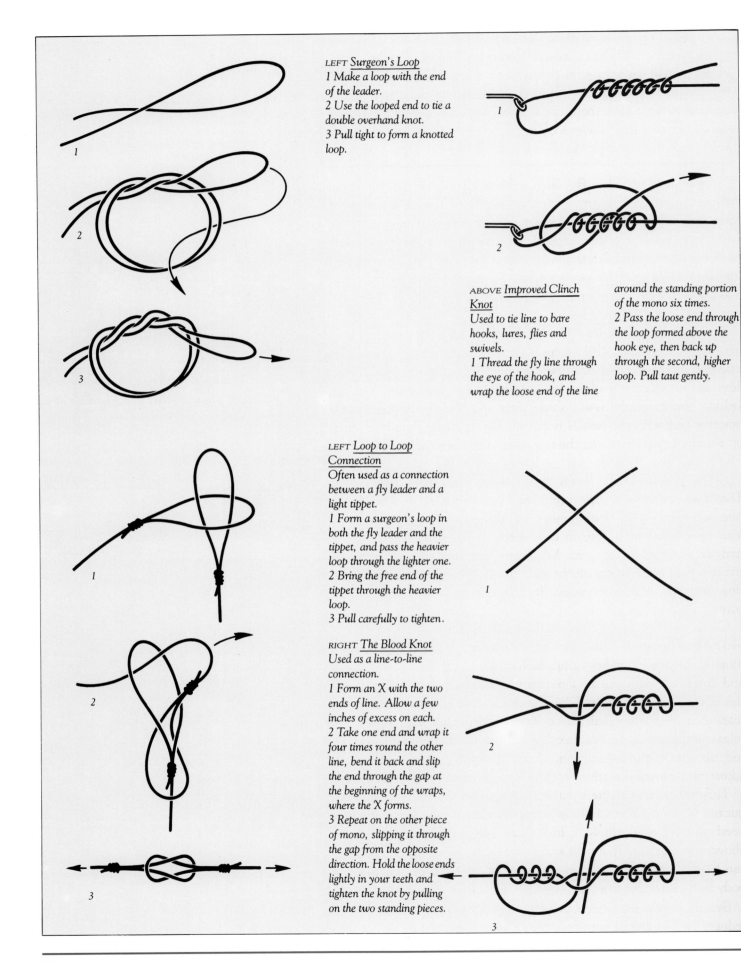

LEFT _Surgeon's Loop_
1 Make a loop with the end of the leader.
2 Use the looped end to tie a double overhand knot.
3 Pull tight to form a knotted loop.

ABOVE _Improved Clinch Knot_
Used to tie line to bare hooks, lures, flies and swivels.
1 Thread the fly line through the eye of the hook, and wrap the loose end of the line around the standing portion of the mono six times.
2 Pass the loose end through the loop formed above the hook eye, then back up through the second, higher loop. Pull taut gently.

LEFT _Loop to Loop Connection_
Often used as a connection between a fly leader and a light tippet.
1 Form a surgeon's loop in both the fly leader and the tippet, and pass the heavier loop through the lighter one.
2 Bring the free end of the tippet through the heavier loop.
3 Pull carefully to tighten.

RIGHT _The Blood Knot_
Used as a line-to-line connection.
1 Form an X with the two ends of line. Allow a few inches of excess on each.
2 Take one end and wrap it four times round the other line, bend it back and slip the end through the gap at the beginning of the wraps, where the X forms.
3 Repeat on the other piece of mono, slipping it through the gap from the opposite direction. Hold the loose ends lightly in your teeth and tighten the knot by pulling on the two standing pieces.

the residual strength of the blood knot. To tie a surgeon's loop, make a loop with the end of the leader. Then use the looped end to tie a double overhand knot, pulling it tight and forming a knotted loop. Tie a second loop in the leader section you wish to attach to the first. To make a loop-to-loop connection, such as between a fly leader and light tippet, pass the heavier loop through the lighter one, then bring the free end of the tippet through the heavier loop and pull to tighten.

Casting

Beginning fishermen have the mistaken notion that long casts are the sign of a good angler. For the most part, they are wrong. Almost anyone can quickly learn to heave a line long distances. But in fishing, the ability to make long casts is of less value than the ability to make accurate casts – dropping your fly, lure or bait exactly where you want it, without snagging bushes or scaring the fish.

The only way to develop that kind of skill is to practice. It isn't necessary to waste valuable fishing time with casting drills; one can easily practice on dry land. Use the same rig you fish with, so you develop a familiarity with it, but instead of using a lure with hooks (which will snare the lawn, shade trees and the family dog,) use a practice plug with the trebles removed. For fly-casting practice, snap off the hook point, leaving the rest of the fly intact.

■ CASTING WITH A SPINNING OUTFIT ■

The key to properly casting a spinning outfit is timing – releasing the line at precisely the right moment. Hold the rod in whichever hand feels most comfortable (usually the hand you write with,) with the reel hanging down below the rod. Most spin-fishermen grip the rod with the reel post between the index and middle finger, or the middle and ring fingers – in both cases, so the index finger can reach down to control the line.

Cradle the line in the first joint of the index finger, then open the bail to free the line. Face your target with the rod in front of you, at roughly a 2 o'clock angle. Bring the rod tip back to about 10 o'clock, and in one smooth motion snap it forward to 2 o'clock again, releasing the line just as the tip nears its starting position. If you've timed the release right, the lure will shoot out toward your target zone. If the release comes too soon, the lure will fall behind you; too late, and the rod tip will snap down, slamming the lure in front of you. Simply adjust your timing accordingly.

This standard, over-the-shoulder cast works well in most situations, but not where overhanging vegetation crowds around. Then, you may need to use a side-arm cast. Instead of snapping the rod in an arc above your head, do it at your side, from back to front. Side-arm casts can be made from the side on which you hold the rod, or across the body from the opposite side.

By varying the amount of power in your cast, you can increase or reduce the distance the lure travels. For pinpoint accuracy, some

ABOVE *A quiet pool, dammed by rocks and logs, attracts the attention of a spin-fisherman on a cold, early spring day.*

ABOVE FROM LEFT TO RIGHT
The Forward Cast
1 Start with the line straight out in front, with the rod tip horizontal. Smartly lift the rod.
2 Halt the upward lift at about 2 o'clock.
3 Just as the line straightens out in the air behind you, drive the rod forward to 10 o'clock, throwing the loop toward the target zone.

anglers use the index finger of their casting hand to slow or stop the line, by feathering it as it comes off the reel.

To cast a closed-face spinning reel, hold the rod so the reel is up. Push in the line-release button and hold it – when the button is released, so is the line. The cast itself is the same as with a spinning outfit; when the rod tip comes back to its original position, release the button and the lure will sail off on the cast.

■ CASTING WITH A BAIT-CASTING OUTFIT ■

Using a bait-casting outfit calls for few special casting moves, but requires a different approach to the reel than does spinning.

The cast itself is a simple, over the shoulder motion, with a flip of the wrist at the end to give the lure a final bit of momentum. Controlling the line is the harder part. On older models, thumb pressure had to be applied directly to the spool, both to keep the line from sailing off prematurely, and to slow and stop the spool at the end of the cast, preventing overspin and a tangled backlash. Many newer reels now have thumb bars that negate the need for direct contact with the spool, and so cut down on blisters.

■ FLY CASTING ■

Fly casting is a two-handed operation – one controls the rod, while the other controls the line. Start with the rod held in your casting hand, reel down, and grip on the cork handle with the thumb on top, pointing toward the rod tip. Have 10 or 15 feet of line stripped off the reel and laying straight out in front of you. With your free hand, gently hold the fly line near the reel; after the cast, you'll use this hand to strip the line back in, rather than reeling it, so it is ready for the next cast. In fly-fishing, the reel is used only for line storage.

■ **THE FORWARD CAST** is the most basic move in fly-fishing. Hold the rod at about 9 o'clock. Quickly lift the tip to about 2 o'clock, which

will snap the line off the ground in front of you and throw it over your shoulder in a loop. Just as the loop straightens out behind you, begin the forward part of the cast, stopping the rod at about 10 o'clock. The line will loop forward in response, and then straighten again, dropping the fly to the water. As the line settles, lower the rod tip to 9 o'clock once more.

Bad timing will cause problems. If you start the forward part of the cast before the loop has straightened out behind you, the line will crack like a whip – and probably snap off your fly. If you wait a second too long, on the other hand, the line will lose momentum and drop, fouling your forward cast. The same thing may happen if you don't give your back cast enough power.

To increase the amount of line in the air, make several false casts – that is, don't allow the line to drop to the water, but keep making forward and back casts, paying out a little more line each time with your free hand.

■ **THE SIDE ARM CAST** is a variation on the basic forward cast, which can be used to avoid overhanging trees – either above you or above the fish you're casting to. The mechanics and moves are the same as with a forward cast, but instead of bringing the rod over your head, the arc is made on a more horizontal plane.

■ **THE ROLL CAST** is a good alternative where there is little room for a backcast. Raise the rod to 12 o'clock, letting the line belly at your side. With a powerful snap, bring the rod down to 10 o'clock. The line will roll out in a loop, dropping the fly on target as the loop opens.

In fly-fishing, far more than spinning or bait-casting, the angler must cast in accordance with the water. A dry fly should float naturally with the current, and not be dragged across the surface as the line is pulled by the moving water. Generally, dry flies are presented by casting upstream and across, so the fly drops several feet above the feeding trout. This way, the fly should float drag-free for a short time

ABOVE FROM LEFT TO RIGHT
The Roll Cast
1 Bring the rod tip back over the casting shoulder and allow the line to sag onto the water at your feet.
2 At the moment the line stops sliding back, sweep the rod forward with a crisp snap, aiming it toward the target.
3 The force of the cast will send a tight loop down the line, unrolling as it goes.

as it passes over the fish. Another approach is to carefully move directly upstream from the fish, then make a forward cast. Just before the line touches down, pull back on the rod momentarily, then drop the tip. This so-called "parachute cast" puts lots of slack in the line, which straightens as the current carries the fly over the trout. Because the fish sees the fly before it can see the leader, this cast is very good for selective trout that have grown leader shy.

Wet flies, nymphs and streamers can be fished on a drag-free upstream cast, like dries, but are usually fished across downstream, so the flow pulls the fly across the current at an angle. Wets and nymphs ordinarily require no additional action, but streamers – which imitate active bait fish – should be fished in quick darts and spurts.

"Reading" the water

Fish do not scatter themselves randomly in a lake or stream. Their requirements for many things – the proper water temperature, escape cover, dissolved oxygen, food – all dictate where they will be found and often at what times.

By knowing a little about how fish live, and learning how to interpret the water conditions with those requirements in mind, you can make a fairly accurate guess at where you'll find the best fishing. Collectively, this skill is called "reading the water," and it is one of the essentials of successful angling.

▌STREAMS ▌

Take a trout stream, for example. Most are a series of flat pools and broken water, with undercut banks, protruding roots and large rocks interrupting the flow. The trout that inhabit the stream have to have

certain conditions to survive. The water must be fairly cool and highly oxygenated; that is why trout can't survive in sluggish, warm creeks and ponds. Also, while trout often live in fast-moving streams, they cannot constantly battle the current, or they will burn more energy than they can recover from eating. So, for most of the time, trout will be found where the current slackens – in slow-moving pools, under banks, or behind rocks and logs that break the flow. These are called *holding stations*. Trout also hold just in front of obstructions, because as the current parts to go around a rock, it forms a small area of quiet water on the upstream side.

LEFT *Fast, choppy water may not look promising, but the nooks and crannies near rocks and other obstructions often hold fish.*

BELOW When water rushes into the head of a pool, it picks up dissolved oxygen and carries with it food – two reasons why trout are often found in such locations.

OPPOSITE Structure can be anything that breaks up the monotony of a bare lake bottom – in this case, old pilings, offering refuge for forage fish and game species alike.

ABOVE By reading the water, this fly-fisherman knows where he is most likely to get a strike – around the submerged rocks, alongside the central current and near the overhanging brush at the shore.

Sometimes, the current will bring food right under the trout's nose as it hovers in its holding station. More often, the trout will have to move out into the main flow of the stream to feed, as during a mayfly hatch. During such times, when food is abundant, it pays the fish to fight the current so it can eat. This is the trout's *feeding station*. Generally speaking, the biggest, most dominant trout will take the best feeding station, for example, a deep pocket just where riffles enter the head of a pool.

But let's say you're looking at a long stretch of deep, fast-moving riffles. There are no obvious pockets to hold trout or smallmouth bass. Would it be a waste of time to fish such a stretch? No, because our view from the surface doesn't tell the whole story. Even in fast water, the streambed rocks provide breaks in the current. A trout that hangs right along the bottom, in front of or behind a rock, will find enough respite from the current.

If the trout are rising to a hatch, locating them is as simple as watching for a rise. But fish feed below the surface most of the time, so finding them is a matter of reading the water. On a stream, fish the head of pools, where fast water enters. Fish around obstructions like logs and rocks, both in the eddy behind it and on the upstream side. Try around overhanging banks and tree roots that provide cover for fish. Don't overlook fast water (as too many fishermen do,) because trout may be hanging right along the bottom, waiting to snatch prey that drifts overhead.

LAKES AND PONDS

These waters can be harder to read, because there is no current to give a clue to bottom conditions, and because the depth is much greater. Even so, still-water fish have habitat preferences that a smart angler can use to great advantage.

The bottom features of a body of water are called *structure* : sunken logs and brushpiles, rock ledges, points, drop-offs, weedbeds and the like. On a featureless lake bottom, structure provides a natural gathering place for fish; bait fish stay close because the structure provides escape cover, and game fish use it because of the bait fish, as well as for protection from predators like osprey and otters. A youngster catching bluegills off a dock is, without knowing it, fishing structure.

Lakes – especially deep ones – may also have thermal zones, layers of colder or warmer water. Different species may stay within different thermal zones, or avoid them completely if they are low in oxygen. Sometimes, changing the depth of a lure by as little as one foot – moving the lure from one zone to another – can turn a fishless day into a success.

Places where streams enter the lake, or where springs bubble up through the lake bottom, are usually productive, especially in hot weather when the incoming water is more attractive to the fish being cooler and more highly oxygenated.

Coves and bays can be hotspots for lake fishing. Bass, pike and muskies like the aquatic vegetation that often chokes shallow coves.

Bass can be found among floating lily pads, while submerged weedbeds are good for pike. In the early spring, shallow bays warm faster than the main body of the lake, attracting fish. Overhanging banks and shoreside vegetation may also hold fish; pickerel and bass, for instance, routinely hug the bank, waiting for frogs and other prey items to blunder by.

Where a point of land enters a lake, the contour continues under the water as well. Points often hold fish, as do drop-offs, where large fish can watch the shallows for food, but have the safety of deep water

BELOW Brushpiles and overhanging shrubbery are prime hiding places for bass, pike and pickerel.

close by. Artificial lakes – be they man-made reservoirs or simple beaver ponds – usually have old stream channels cutting through the bed. These channels function like drop-offs, offering fish the concealment of deeper water.

OPPOSITE Early morning and late evening are traditionally considered the best times to fish, even though researchers have found that many fish feed steadily all through the day.

Time, temperature and weather

Conventional wisdom holds that early morning and late evening are the prime times to fish, and that doing so in mid-afternoon is a waste of effort. In many circumstances that is true, but there are plenty of exceptions.

Why are most fish caught early and late? It may have something to

ABOVE *Nightfall is one of the most productive times to fish, especially for trophies that skulk in deep water during the day, but move into the shallows to feed after dark.*

OPPOSITE *An incoming storm, with its strong winds and rapidly falling barometric pressure, can spark furious feeding – sometimes. Weather's effect on fishing can be capricious, and is difficult to predict.*

do with the angle of the sun; when the sun is high in the sky, visibility through the water is greatest, exposing the fish to airborne predators like kingfishers, ospreys and terns. When the sun is low, fish seem to be less cautious about moving actively, especially away from cover, making them more likely to be found. Also, some fish like walleye and catfish are primarily nocturnal, and may spend the hours in the middle of the day resting.

But researchers who have studied fish behaviour have found that many species, such as brown trout, feed freely throughout the day. It may be that more fish are caught in the morning and evening simply because that's when most people are fishing for them.

Night fishing can be exceptionally rewarding, especially for trophy fish. Instead of sulking beneath fallen logs and in deep water, predatory fish are on the move, hunting the shallows they avoid by day. Night is the prime time for big walleye, bass, catfish, brown trout and muskies – even moonless nights when vision is almost useless. Fish are much less reliant on their eyes than are humans. Instead, they use a number of senses to tell them what is happening around them – sound, odor, and especially vibrations in the water which are detected by a sensitive system of nerve endings. A crude analogy would be to liken the fish's senses to a submarine's sonar, detecting movement, discriminating between random motion and that of prey. In fact, fish operate at a much higher level of sophistication than anything people have invented.

RIGHT Depending on the species sought, winter fishing can be quite rewarding, especially for trout in spring-fed streams that stay somewhat warmer through the cold weather.

© JOE REYNOLDS

Water temperature plays a greater role in determining the catch than many fishermen realize. Fish have an optimum temperature range, within which their bodies function at peak efficiency. Because they are cold-blooded, fish are at the mercy of the thermometer far more than warm-blooded mammals. If the water is colder than their optimum range, they will be sluggish and have little appetite. If it gets too warm, the fish suffer not just from the heat, but usually from decreased oxygen in the water. The result is the same – sluggishness and very little feeding. If the temperature climbs too high above the optimum, the fish may actually die.

Each species has a different optimum range, and knowing it may help your fishing. During early spring, when snowmelt chills streams, brook trout will be lethargic until the water warms to about 52°F, and will eat most freely when the stream is between 57°F and 60°F. Large-mouth bass, on the other hand, can tolerate temperatures in the 80s and higher. Bluegills, oddly, may feed as aggressively beneath a sheet of ice as they do on a balmy summer's day.

Fishermen have long known that weather affects fishing dramatically. Bright, blue skies and high pressure are the nicest days to fish, but are often the worst in terms of catching something. An approaching low pressure system and cold front, on the other hand, may spark furious feeding. It is impossible, though, to predict exactly how a particular weather pattern will impact on the fishing. A bright, sunny day in early spring may be just the thing to warm up a stream and nudge the trout into feeding. A sudden downpour may turn the fish off, or it may inject new life into a dull day.

ABOVE *Bright, blue-sky days may be the most pleasant for anglers, but they can be difficult to fish – the bright sun and high air pressure often dampen feeding.*

LEFT *At dusk, a fisherman coaxes in a trophy Canadian brook trout.*

© JOE REYNOLDS

ABOVE *A smallmouth bass rockets into the air at boatside. During the fight, keep the rod tip high so it – and not the delicate line – absorbs the shock of unexpected lunges.*

The effect weather has on fishing can also vary with the species being sought. Heavy overcast skies may keep walleye, which feed at night, active on through the day. Blustery winds that create a chop on a lake might ruin the bass fishing, but such conditions are often ideal for pike.

Playing a fish

The most electrifying moment in fishing is that instant when the fish strikes. Line rips off the reel, the rod bucks and the fish leaps high. What you do in those first seconds may determine whether you take a prize – or a sad story – back home with you.

Playing a fish is a delicate contest. Too much pressure on the line and it may break; not enough, and the fish may bulldog its way into thick cover, snarling the line and snapping free, or throw the hook. That uncertainty adds much of the suspense and challenge to fishing.

The strike may be subtle or ferocious, depending on the mood and appetite of the fish. A trout that is rising to mayflies, which are slow to fly from the water's surface, will usually sip them down delicately. Caddisflies, on the other hand, take wing the instant they reach the top, and so during a caddis hatch the rises may be wild and slashing, with fish even jumping clear of the water to grab an escaping fly.

LEFT A critical moment in the fight: a salmon thrashes on a short line, and a moment's carelessness will mean a snapped line and a lost fish.

A fish that grabs a lure or bait may hook itself, especially in moving water, but it is far better to make a conscious effort to set the hook. In most cases, all that is needed is to raise the rod tip, exerting firm pressure on the line and driving the hook point home. Don't get carried away; too much sudden pressure may break the line, especially if you're using light tackle. A few fish with bony mouths, like pike and muskellunge, may require a more vigorous set.

Once the fish is on, the rod and reel work together during the fight to absorb the strain of sudden tension on the line – the rod by flexing, the reel by giving up line at a rate determined by the drag setting. During the fight, keep the rod tip high; if you lower it, all the pressure is on the line, which may break. Also, keeping the tip up makes the fish fight against the power of the rod, thus tiring it faster.

Set the drag according to the fish you're after. Light drag – a setting that allows line to be pulled easily from the closed reel – is good for panfish and other smaller species. For larger fish, obviously, the drag must be tightened, or the fish will peel off more mono than you can recover from reeling. If, in the middle of a fight, you discover that your drag setting is wrong, keep the rod tip up and adjust the drag control accordingly.

The basic rule for playing fish was summed up well many years ago: When the fish pulls, you don't. When it doesn't, you do. Never try to heave a strong fish to shore – it's an invitation to a broken line or hooks pulled loose. When the fish makes a run, keep steady pressure on it from the rod tip, but wait until the run is over before trying to recover line. If the fish bolts toward fast water or thick cover, try angling the rod away from its direction of travel. Usually, such a maneuver will turn the fish away from danger.

Most fish tire rather quickly. When the fight begins to diminish, work the fish to shore to land it. If you're using a net, put it in the water and lead the fish into it, head first. Never try to scoop a fish, or come up from behind with the net – both ways will force the fish into a final run, and a mistimed scoop may snap your line.

A net is convenient, but hardly essential for any but the biggest fish. Most can be landed just as well by beaching – that is, easing the fish onto a shallow, sloping shore – or by hand. Be careful, though, not to lift the fish out of the water supported by just the line; in air, it weighs more than underwater, and a last flop may spell disaster for the line or hook.

Trout fishermen usually land fish by easing their hand under the fish's belly, then gently lifting it from the water. Held like that, a trout stays fairly quiet while the hook is being removed. Bass can be "lipped," grabbed by their lower jaw and lifted from the water, but be careful to avoid treble hooks. Pike and other toothy species obviously can't be lipped; use a net if you can, but in a pinch, grasp the pike just behind the gills, then lift it into the boat.

If you're going to eat the fish, slip it onto a stringer or in a live well. Be a good conservationist; if you won't eat it, gently release it for someone else to enjoy. Such catch-and-release fishing is growing in

BELOW *A fly-fisherman carefully nets a trophy brown trout, leading it head first into the net with gentle rod pressure.*

OPPOSITE *A glove is a good idea for hand-landing northern pike, which have sharp gill rakers that can slash any fingers that slip inside the gill plates.*

ABOVE *Bass, like this largemouth, can be easily landed by gripping the lower lip and lifting. Be careful, however, to avoid the lure's hooks, especially if they are trebles.*

ABOVE By gripping the tail base and supporting its stomach, even large trout like this Alaskan rainbow can be landed, unhooked and returned to the water unharmed.

popularity among enlightened anglers who realize that a heavy stringer is not the true measure of a day well spent.

How you fight, land and handle a fish will largely determine whether it will survive after release. Don't play a fish to exhaustion; it isn't necessary, and the buildup of toxins in its muscles – an unavoidable consequence of fighting – will kill it in short order. Handle the fish with wet hands to protect its vital slime coat, and avoid squeezing it, which can cause serious internal damage. After it's unhooked, return it gently to the water rather than simply tossing it back with a splash. Hold it upright and allow it to swim away under its own power. If the fish seems very weak, or if it can't maintain its equilibrium, hold it loosely by the tail until it recovers. In moving water, always release a fish facing upstream, so the water flows through the gills properly.

Fish are a natural resource, and fishermen have a responsibility to conserve them for the future. If you plan to release your catch, consider using only artificial lures, rather than bait that is often swallowed entirely. Barbless hooks also minimize damage, and reduce the time it takes to unhook the fish.

LEFT A steelhead, netted and unhooked, is eased back into the current. By gripping the base of the tail, the angler maintains control while not injuring the fish or damaging its essential slime coating.

OPPOSITE Lake maps are often available in bait and tackle shops, or from state fishing agencies. They show submerged structure, lake depths and other essential information.

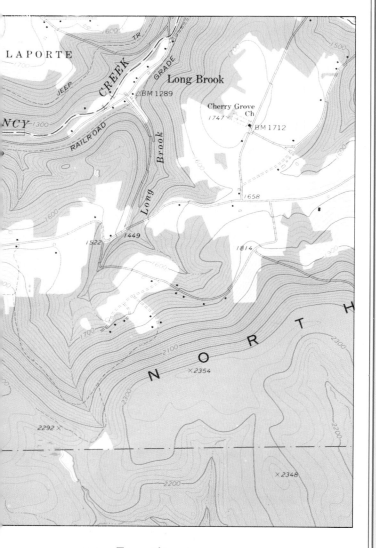

ABOVE Topographic maps provide a wealth of information about terrain, forest cover and waterways, and can help pinpoint new fishing spots, like this isolated mountaintop pond.

DOING YOUR HOMEWORK

Maps can be invaluable to fishermen – not just road maps to guide you to the lake, but specialized maps that can lead you to new hotspots or show you around unfamiliar waters. A little homework, specially during winter, can pay big dividends later.

Start with topographic maps, published by the U.S. Geological Survey. "Topos" are highly detailed maps that show the physical features of the land – the hills, cliffs, lakes, marshes, forests and fields, as well as roads and towns. They can reveal previously unknown waters, particularly in mountainous areas. Such remote streams and lakes are usually underfished, and can provide some spectacular fishing for those anglers willing to hike in.

The most important aspect of a topo map are its contour lines, the brown, parallel lines that indicate the grade of hills and height above sea level. Depending on the map series, the contour interval may be 10, 20 or 40 feet: in other words, on a 20-foot-interval map, the vertical distance between contour lines is 20 feet. If the lines are spaced widely, the slope is gentle. If the lines are packed close together, expect to find hard going.

The most common topo series is the 7.5-minute series. Each map – called a quadrangle, or quad – covers an area roughly 6½ miles by 8½ miles. Each quad is named for a local town or landmark. To order, write to: U.S. Geological Survey at either the Eastern Distribution Branch, 1200 S. Eads St., Arlington, Va. 22202, or the Western Distribution Branch, Box 25286, Federal Center, Denver, CO 80225. Ask for the brochure describing the quads for the state in which you are interested. Old topo maps can be useful in figuring the best places to fish man-made reservoirs. Former stream channels, road beds, drop-offs and points that are hidden by the new dam will all show up on maps that predate its construction. For some popular fishing lakes, underwater maps showing the major submerged features may be available at near-by tackle and bait shops. While usually not as accurate as government maps, they can guide you in the right general direction.

State or provincial fish and game agencies – whose business it is, after all, to help fishermen catch fish – are usually a treasure-trove of information that can help you plan upcoming trips. Most agencies have a department of information or public affairs, which will gladly supply you with a list of publications that detail where and when to go for particular species of gamefish, where to find public boat ramps and much, much more.

Local conservation officers can also be of tremendous help. These dedicated men and women spend much of their time in the field, talking to sportsmen, and know not just where the best fishing is found, but usually also the lures or bait that are currently working.

Periodically, man-made lakes are drained, either completely or partially, for repair work or to control aquatic vegetation. Such draw-downs actually improve fishing in later years, and provide anglers with a rare opportunity to learn the lay of the land. Draw your own maps of the lake floor, noting channels, stumps, sunken logs, rockpiles, old roads – anything that would attract fish once the lake is refilled. It is obviously important to note nearby surface features as well, so you can find the structure when the waters again rise.

Chapter Three

THE
QUARRY

T r o u t   a n d   s a l m o n

Perhaps the epitome of freshwater fish, the members of the family Salmonidae are renowned for their intelligence, beauty and fight. Coldwater fish, they require exceptionally clean rivers, streams and lakes, and all except the Atlantic salmon are stocked far beyond their original ranges.

▮ BROOK TROUT ▮

North American record: 14lb 8oz; Nipigon River, Ontario 1916.

▪ **RANGE:** Originally East, heavily stocked in West.

▪ **HABITAT:** Very cold streams, rivers and lakes.

▪ **MAIN FOODS:** Aquatic and terrestrial insects, minnows, invertebrates. In a sense, there are really three kinds of brook trout: the pale hatchery fish stocked by wildlife agencies, the small, brilliantly colored native trout of mountain streams across the East, and the big, brawling monsters of the far north.

In each case, the pattern is unmistakable, making a brook trout the easiest to identify. On a fish of good color, the back will be green, marbled with lighter vermiculations that snake like worm trails over the fish's upper side. The flanks will be spotted with red dots, each surrounded with a circlet of blue, and the red fins will be edged with stripes of black and white.

Of all the trout, the brookie requires the coldest water, restricting self-sustaining populations to chilly mountain creeks and lakes. The brookie was originally an Easterner, found naturally from the Georgia mountains to Canada. It has been widely stocked, however, and wild brook trout are common in many western waters.

Brook trout have a reputation for being perhaps the least wary of North American trout, a belief that is true only in food-poor waters, like the small, fast creeks where they are often found. In spring creeks, or where they are subjected to heavy fishing pressure, brooks can become every bit as selective as other trout.

▮ BROWN TROUT ▮

North American record: 34lb 6oz; Bar Lake, Michigan, 1984.

▪ **RANGE:** European native, stocked widely.

▪ **HABITAT:** Streams, cool rivers and lakes.

▪ **MAIN FOODS:** Aquatic and terrestrial insects, smaller fish, crayfish. Once condemned as a cannibalistic trash fish, the brown trout has been the salvation of trout fishing in many areas of the U.S., where pollution, sedimentation and warming waters wiped out the brook trout. Introduced from Europe in the 1880s over the heated objections of many fishermen, the brown trout is today one of the most widely distributed trout, a particular favorite of the fly-fishermen because of its almost legendary selectivity.

Wild or hold-over stocked brown trout are usually a beautiful golden color, speckled with black (and sometimes red) spots on the

OPPOSITE *The brook trout was the original native trout of the East, where it is still found wild in mountain streams, and the far north. It has been stocked widely in the past century, and can now be caught across much of the continent.*

ABOVE *A Great Lakes brown trout exhibits the deep, powerful body and silvery coloration that this species develops in big water. Browns in rivers and streams tend to develop a rich, golden color.*

ABOVE A wide band of crimson gives the rainbow trout its name. Stocked fish are often much paler, and are best told from brown trout by the hundreds of fine dots that cover the entire fish, including the tail.

body. Among hatchery fish the body color may be silver, making them difficult to separate from stocked rainbow trout, but rainbows usually have heavily spotted tails, a feature absent from most browns.

Even stocked brown trout quickly key into the insect life of their stream or lake, feeding heavily on nymphs most of the day, and on adult mayflies, caddis and stoneflies during hatches. As they grow, browns turn increasingly to fish for their food, and the largest are generally taken on minnow imitations.

▌ RAINBOW TROUT ▌

North American record (steelhead form): 42lb 2oz; Bell Island, Alaska, 1970.

■ **RANGE:** Originally West, now widely stocked.

■ **HABITAT:** Clean lakes, streams and rivers; also a sea-run form.

■ **MAIN FOODS:** Small fish, insects, invertebrates.

The rainbow trout is the aerialist of the family, leaping and splashing as soon as the hook is felt, fighting with a gusto that has earned the admiration of millions of anglers. Other trout may jump, but the rainbow does so with a vigor and stamina that adds untold excitement to the catch.

Rainbows come in two forms – the standard landlocked variety, native to the West but stocked today in almost every nook of North America; and the large, sea-run steelhead, which like the salmon spends several years in saltwater before returning to its home river to spawn. They can be monstrous; the all-tackle record for a steelhead was more than 42 pounds, from coastal Alaska. Steelhead were once a speciality of the Northwest, but plantings in the Great Lakes during the 1960s and '70s have produced a fantastic steelhead fishery there, as well.

Landlocked rainbows get their name from the crimson band that runs down the fish's side – a stripe that may be absent in hatchery fish, which are usually much paler than wild trout.

LEFT A lake trout surfaces to unaccustomed sunshine from the gloomy depths where this species normally spends most of its life.

▌ LAKE TROUT ▌

North American record: 65lb; Great Bear Lake, Northwest Territories, 1970.

▪ **RANGE:** Canada, Alaska, Great Lakes, New England; stocked in West and some northern areas.

▪ **HABITAT:** Very deep, cold lakes.

▪ **MAIN FOODS:** Fish.

Catching lake trout is a game played in the North Country, in icy, glacial lakes where these huge fish school in the deepest water, frequently 150 or more feet down. Anglers must use specialized equipment, including lead- core lines and downriggers, simply to take their lures deep enough. Large spoons and minnow-shaped plugs bring the best results.

Lake trout are the largest landlocked salmonids, routinely reaching weight of 15 or 20 pounds, and commercial fishermen have netted giants of more than 100 pounds. Lake trout have deeply forked tails, dark fins and greenish bodies covered with hundreds of large, white spots.

Once abundant in the Great Lakes, lake trout were decimated by overfishing, pollution and lamprey predation. Artificial propagation and stocking, however, are restoring these populations.

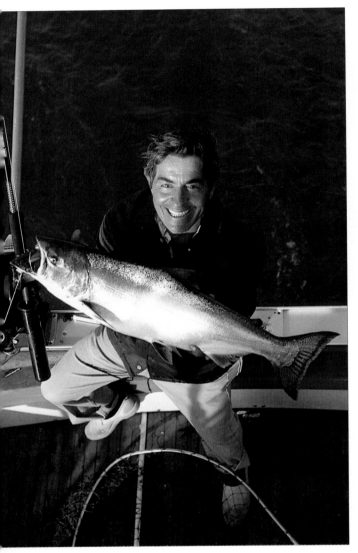

BELOW The chinook, or king, salmon is the heaviest of the five species of Pacific salmon, reaching weights well in excess of 60 pounds. While landlocked specimens like this one do not grow as large, they are still tremendous game fish.

▌ CUTTHROAT TROUT ▌

North American record: 41lb; Pyramid Lake, Nevada, 1925.

■ **RANGE:** Western U.S. and Canada.

■ **HABITAT:** Rivers, streams and lakes.

■ **MAIN FOODS:** Aquatic insects and freshwater shrimp.

John Skimmerhorn's 41-pound cutthroat will probably never be matched, because the unique, monster strain from Pyramid Lake is now gone. Elsewhere, this species generally doesn't achieve the heavy weights that rainbows and browns can reach, and in most waters, a 5-pound cutt is a lifetime trophy – and a beautiful one at that.

More so than other trout, the cutthroat has developed distinct races, isolated in specific river drainages and each colored differently than the others. The Snake River cutthroat, for instance, is a rich golden-brown, speckled with fine black dots. The Yellowstone cutthroat, on the other hand, is greenish, with larger spots. All, however, share the cutthroat trademark, a bright red or orange slash mark beneath each jaw.

Some of the best Western fishing is for native cutthroats, in large rivers like the Yellowstone and in thousands of smaller streams. Many alpine lakes, once devoid of fish because they are not connected to streams, have been stocked with cutts, providing excellent backcountry fishing.

In many waters, freshwater shrimp are a prime cutthroat food, coupled with mayflies, stoneflies, caddis and such terrestrial insects as grasshoppers.

▌ CHINOOK SALMON ▌

North American record: 97lb 4oz; Kenai River, Alaska, 1985.

■ **RANGE:** Pacific Ocean, running up rivers from California to Alaska. Stocked inland, especially in Great Lakes.

■ **HABITAT:** Enters large rivers, often ascending them for hundreds of miles.

■ **MAIN FOODS:** Fasts during spawning run; eats fish, squid and crabs at sea, small fish in lakes.

In many areas, the chinook salmon is known as the king salmon – a fitting name for a game fish that reaches such astounding weights. It is one of the premier sport fish in North America, capable of smashing even the strongest gear.

The chinook is one of five Pacific salmon species, although together with the coho only these two species are considered important game fish. Spawning males develop a deep, red color and hooked jaws, as do other salmon; the best way to separate chinooks and coho is to look at the gums – black in chinooks, but with white at the base of the teeth in cohos.

A good chinook fishery has developed in the Great Lakes, where this species was stocked in the 1960s. Angling is done with downriggers in deep water most of the year, and with spinning and fly gear during the spawning runs. In most areas the eggs do not survive natural spawning, so annual stocking of fry keeps the fishery going.

▌ COHO SALMON ▌

North American record: 31lb; Cowichan Bay, British Columbia, 1947.

▪ **RANGE:** Pacific coast from California north; stocked in Great Lakes, elsewhere.

▪ **HABITAT:** Rivers and large streams during run, in late summer through early winter.

▪ **MAIN FOODS:** Fasts during spawning run; eats fish, squid, crabs, plankton at sea, fish in lakes.

Also known as the silver salmon, the coho is a hard fighter that leaps

BELOW The coho salmon, also known as the silver, has thrived in the Great Lakes as well as its native Pacific Northwest.

repeatedly when hooked in shallow water, putting on a spectacular show. Couple that with the salmon's size – up to 15 or 20 pounds – and it is no wonder that cohos are eagerly sought by anglers.

Stocked as an experiment in the Great Lakes, cohos thrived on the lakes' abundant bait fish, growing fat and sparking a tremendous fishery. Using downriggers, fishermen pursue schools of salmon year-round, but the excitement builds in late summer, when the fish begin congregating near the mouths of tributary streams. Through the fall, anglers from shore and along the spawning creeks are treated to unexcelled fishing. Like all salmon, cohos do not eat during their spawning run, but will hit spoons, plugs, spinners and flies, perhaps from a latent feeding reflex.

▌ ATLANTIC SALMON ▌

International record: 79lb 2oz; Tana River, Norway, 1928.
▪ **RANGE:** In North America, northern New England and eastern Canada.
▪ **HABITAT:** Spawns in cold, pure rivers. Landlocked form in some inland lakes.
▪ **MAIN FOODS:** Fasts during spawning run.

BELOW The Atlantic salmon is the monarch of fly-fishing – an elusive species of wilderness rivers, it summons immense strength when hooked.

Perhaps the most revered game fish in the world, the Atlantic salmon is inextricably linked with fly-fishing; indeed, some of the most beautiful flies ever made – gorgeous, multi-colored creations of exotic feathers – were designed for this fish.

Pollution and dams have severely curtailed Atlantic salmon populations on the Northeast coast, and almost all serious fishing is done in coastal Canada, where rivers like the Restigouche have achieved fame for their salmon fishing.

Atlantic salmon are not closely related to Pacific salmon, and unlike them do not always die after spawning. Males develop a hooked jaw, or kype, but retain much of their slim form and silvery-bronze color. An inland form, the landlocked salmon, or ouananiche, inhabits deep lakes in Maine, and has been stocked in several other states. It does not achieve the large size of its sea-going relatives, rarely growing to more than 2 or 3 pounds.

Walleye, pike and muskellunge

Similar in shape, range and habitat, walleyes and the members of the pike family are prized game fish, both on the line and in the pan.

▮ WALLEYE ▮

North American record: 25lb; Old Hickory Lake, Tennessee, 1960.

■ **RANGE:** Originally northern, now stocked in all but extreme South and parts of West.

■ **HABITAT:** Deep, cold lakes; also in some rivers and large streams.

■ **MAIN FOODS:** Fish, some crayfish and invertebrates.

When the sun drops and the lake darkens, the walleye schools move out of the deep water and begin to feed, hunting down minnows through the night, seeing through the gloom with their weird, glassy eyes. When morning returns, the schools will sink back to deeper water, or hang in the shadows of shoreside cliffs and hills.

Averaging 2-5 pounds, and occasionally topping out at 10, the walleye is a long, slim fish, brassy-gold in color with dark, vertical bars. The wide mouth is studded with small, very sharp teeth, and the front dorsal fin has spines that help to protect it from pike. The walleye is very popular with anglers, even though it is, frankly, better to eat than to play, being a rather sluggish fighter. The flesh makes up for any lack, though – firm, sweet and very good. A very similar fish, the sauger, is found in the Greak Lakes and central U.S.

▮ NORTHERN PIKE ▮

International record: 55lb 1oz; West Germany 1986.

■ **RANGE:** In North America, primarily northern U.S. and most of Canada, but widely stocked in South and West.

■ **HABITAT:** Lakes with weedy coves and abundant structure.

■ **MAIN FOODS:** Primarily fish, but will eat almost anything, including frogs, snakes, muskrats and even ducks.

At times, a pike seems like nothing more than a mouth with an appetite attached. They are voracious feeders, gorging on whatever fate brings their way – one of the reasons they are among the fastest-growing game fish in North America.

So sinuous that many North Country natives call them "snakes," pike are long and slim, with one small dorsal fin just ahead of the tail. Pike are generally greenish-yellow, with hundreds of lighter, oval-shaped spots on the body. The flat, duckbill-shaped mouth is an armory of needle-sharp teeth, covering even the upper palate. In remote northern lakes , trophies of 15–25 pounds are not uncommon, although most pike caught are in the 5- to 10-pound range.

On the prowl, a pike drifts imperceptibly through weed-choked bays, looking very much like a log – until it is within striking distance of its prey. Then the cavernous mouth opens, and the hapless fish or frog disappears in a swirl of water.

BELOW *Light reflects off the odd, silvery eye of a walleye, caught on a rubber-and-marabou jig.*

ABOVE *A big northern pike is displayed against a tacklebox full of the large, brightly colored lures that work well for this predaceous species.*

RIGHT Chain pickerel and a lone yellow perch fill this stringer. Pickerel have the lean shape of their larger cousin, the northern pike, but rarely exceed 15 inches.

OPPOSITE With a heave, a fisherman nets a muskellunge, one of the biggest freshwater game fish on the continent – and perhaps the hardest to catch.

▌ CHAIN PICKEREL ▌

North American record: 9lb 6oz; Homerville, Georgia, 1961.

■ **RANGE:** Eastern U.S. and southeastern Canada.

■ **HABITAT:** Weedy ponds and lakes; some streams.

■ **MAIN FOODS:** Fish, frogs, invertebrates.

A small version of the pike in appearance, food and habits, the pickerel rarely grows larger than 15 or 20 inches, and most that are caught are considerably smaller.

The pickerel has the same slim profile as the pike, but is lighter in color, with an interlocking network of dark lines – the "chain" of its name. It is common in small ponds and lakes, lurking where cover is the heaviest, using a wait-and-see technique in its hunting. Minnows are its mainstay food, which explains why bright spinners frequently work so well for them.

▌ MUSKELLUNGE ▌

North American record: 69lb 15oz; St. Lawrence River, 1957.

■ **RANGE:** Great Lake and upper Midwest, Ohio River drainage and southeastern Canada.

■ **HABITAT:** Lakes and slow-moving sections of rivers.

■ **MAIN FOODS:** Fish, particularly perch; also reptiles, amphibians, crayfish, small mammals and waterbirds.

Muskellunge are perhaps the hardest North American game fish to catch. Many anglers fish a lifetime in muskie country without ever boating one, and those who specialize in hunting them are resigned to spending hundreds of hours for each trophy they catch.

The reason, in part, is the muskellunge's low population density in most lakes, but part also seems to be a simple lack of willingness to strike, unlike the free-biting northern pike.

Muskies reach very large size, with many in the 40-pound class taken each year. Their shape is almost exactly like a pike's, but the body color is brownish, often with indistinct vertical bars or spotting. The two species can easily be confused, and the most reliable difference is the scaling on the gill cover: completely scaled in pike, only half covered in muskies.

Muskies are usually taken by casting or trolling very big, minnow-shaped plugs, or by bait-fishing with large – up to 12 inch – suckers and chubs. Muskellunge hunt in typical pike fashion, staying close to weedbeds where they are available.

S h a d

Of the four species of Shad in North America, only two, the American shad and the hickory shad, are major game fish. The smaller gizzard and threadfin shad are important forage fish for larger species.

■ AMERICAN SHAD ■

North American record: 11lb 4oz; Connecticut River, Massachusetts, 1986.

■ **RANGE:** East coast from Florida to Canada; stocked in Western rivers.

■ **HABITAT:** Sea-going like salmon; spawning runs up large rivers.

■ **MAIN FOODS:** Fasts in freshwater; eats plankton at sea.

The shad is a fish with little glory, although more and more anglers are discovering that this sea-going relative of the herring is a superior sport fish.

The spawning run begins in spring, peaking in May on the Delaware River between Pennsylvania and New Jersey, a popular fishing spot. First the males, or "bucks," come upstream, followed later by the "roes," or egg-laden females. American shad average 6 to 10 pounds, with a deep, flattened body, delicate mouth and forked tail. They are plain silver, with a few dark spots behind the eye.

Shad fishermen rely on lead-headed lures called darts, painted in a variety of bright colors and dressed with colored bucktail. The darts are fished suspended in the current, to intercept migrating schools of shad, which apparently strike on reflex. Why they should do so is a mystery, because they do not feed while on the spawning run, and even their natural food, plankton, looks nothing like a dart. When hooked, shad take off on sizzling runs, punctuated with repeated jumps.

P a n f i s h

These are the bread-and-butter fish of North American angling, fairly easy to catch, found almost everywhere and as a bonus, they are excellent eating. The term "panfish" is broadly applied to many different fish, including bass, sunfish, catfish and carp.

ABOVE *A stringer of bluegills – the result of fun fishing, and the promise of good eating to come.*

▌ BLUEGILL ▌

North American record: 4lb 12oz; Ketona Lake, Alabama, 1950.

▌ **RANGE:** Virtually all the U.S., and parts of Canada.

▌ **HABITAT:** Farm ponds, lakes, sluggish streams and rivers.

▌ **MAIN FOODS:** Insects, invertebrates.

The bluegill has probably introduced more anglers to fishing than any other species in North America. The classic image of a kid with a cane pole, bobber and a can of worms isn't complete with a stringer of bluegills, or bream, as they are known in the South.

Actually, most fishermen indiscriminately apply the name bluegill to almost any of the dozens of species of sunfish found on the continent, almost all of which share a small spot of blue at the back edge of each gill plate. Bluegills are one of the largest of the family, and if predators keep them from overpopulating the lake they can grow to more than a foot.

In spring, the males stake out territories in shallow water, where the pairs make saucer-shaped nests in the mud and gravel. A male will jealously guard the eggs, and later the fry, from intruders, but the females leave after spawning.

▌ WHITE CRAPPIE AND BLACK CRAPPIE ▌

North American records: White – 5lb 3oz; Enid Dam, Mississippi, 1957. Black – 4lb 8oz; Kerr Dam, Virginia, 1981.

▌ **RANGE:** With stocking, almost continent-wide.

▌ **HABITAT:** Lakes; black crappie prefers colder, clearer water.

▌ **MAIN FOODS:** Minnows; also insects and invertebrates.

A favorite game fish in many areas, crappie (known as crappie bass or croppie in some areas) are fish-eaters that readily take spinners, jigs and other minnow imitations. When the crappie strikes at prey, it opens its large, funnel-shaped mouth, creating momentary suction that pulls the minnow in. The mouth is thin and delicate, however, and fishermen must be careful to play a crappie gently. Even so, many pull free before being boated.

Members of the sunfish family, black and white crappie are so similar that few anglers bother to tell one from the other. Generally, the black crappie inhabits colder waters, and has dark speckles that sometimes form horizontal blotches. The white has the same basically silver body color, but with vertical barring instead of spots. In most waters, 1 or 2 pounds is the average size.

Crappie often school around brushpiles and other submerged structure, where vertical jigging can produce plenty of action.

▌ LARGEMOUTH BASS ▌

North American record: 22lb 4oz; Montgomery Lake, Georgia, 1932.

▌ **RANGE:** Almost universal from southern Canada on south.

▌ **HABITAT:** Warm, weedy lakes, ponds, sluggish rivers.

▌ **MAIN FOODS:** Fish, frogs, insects, snakes, crayfish, invertebrates, small mammals.

ABOVE *A happy angler hefts a nice black crappie. The very similar white crappie has spots that form vertical bars, and will tolerate muddier waters than the black.*

To millions of anglers, the largemouth bass is the only fish worth pursuing, and they do so with a fervor, investing in expensive bass boats and an arsenal of tackle.

The object of their zeal is found in virtually every corner of the U.S. and southern Canada, from farm ponds and reservoirs to rivers, streams and even tidal areas. Depending on the water, largemouths average 2–5 pounds, with Southern trophy fish reaching 10 or 12. Greenish, with a big head and a dark line running down each side, the largemouth is easily confused with its cool-water relative, the smallmouth, especially when both bass occur in the same lake or river. When the mouth is closed, the largemouth's jaw extends back *beyond* the rear of the eye. In smallmouths, the jaw comes only to the middle of the eye.

Largemouths are ambush hunters, hiding in the cover of aquatic vegetation, brushpiles, docks and stumps until food comes by. The attack may come in a slashing rush, or only after the bass has followed its prey for quite a distance. In the spring, when the males are defending their plate-sized nests, scooped out of the lake bottom, anything that comes too close will be grabbed. For this reason, most states delay the opening of bass season until after spawning is over.

▮ SMALLMOUTH BASS ▮

North American record: 11lb 15oz; Dale Hollow Lake, Kentucky, 1955.

▪ **RANGE:** Stocked widely; now found in most of U.S. and southern Canada.

▪ **HABITAT:** Prefers cool water, in lakes, rivers or streams.

▪ **MAIN FOODS:** Small fish, crayfish, insects, frogs.

A hooked smallmouth seems to spend more time dancing in the air than swimming. Red gills flaring, it will leap and tail-walk all the way to the boat, if it doesn't throw the hook first.

The smallmouth prefers colder waters than the largemouth, and as a consequence it is not as ubiquitous. It is equally at home in cool lakes or in moving water. In fact, some of the best smallmouth fishing is in rivers, like Pennsylvania's Susquehanna, or Virginia's James.

Although the smallmouth and largemouth have the same basic shape, the smallmouth tends to be slimmer, lacking the barrel-shaped belly many largemouths develop. Older fish have a beautiful, brassy color to the back and sides (hence the common nickname, "bronzeback",) and usually have vertical brown barring, instead of the largemouth's lateral stripe.

Where they are abundant, crayfish form a major part of the smallmouth's diet, supplemented with minnows and such aquatic insects as the hellgramites and stoneflies.

RIGHT The brassy colors of a pair of smallmouth bass nicely compliment the red maple leaves of autumn – a prime time for bass fishing.

YELLOW PERCH

North American record: 4lb 3oz; Bordentown, New Jersey, 1865.

■ **RANGE:** Northern Canada south to the Carolinas; stocked in many other areas.

■ **HABITAT:** Cool lakes.

■ **MAIN FOODS:** Insects, invertebrates, small fish.

The yellow perch is an attractive fish – golden yellow, fading to white toward the belly, with dark greenish bars and bright orange ventral fins. Where it is abundant it can be a pest, stealing the bait meant for larger fish, but it is an excellent food fish.

Perch are a major prey species for many larger fish, like pike, muskellunge and walleye, and congregate in large schools for protection. Nevertheless, predators exact a terrible toll, and as many as 80 percent may perish in their first year. Those that survive, however, may grow to lengths of about a foot, and weights of a pound or two; the fact that the world record has stood since the mid-1800s is an indication that perch rarely get much bigger.

WHITE BASS AND YELLOW BASS

North American records: White – 5lb 14oz; Kerr Dam, North Carolina, 1986. Yellow – 2lb 4oz; Lake Monroe, Indiana, 1977.

■ **RANGE:** White – Great Lakes and Midwest south to Texas; Yellow – Upper Midwest and Ohio Valley, stocked in South and Southwest.

■ **HABITAT:** Large lakes; yellow bass also in some rivers.

■ **MAIN FOODS:** Insects, aquatic invertebrates and small fish.

Although not large, these two related species enjoy tremendous popularity because of their abundance and sporting qualities.

White and yellow bass are built along very similar lines – high arched back, two dorsal fins and jutting lower jaws. White bass are the larger fish and silvery, with thin, parallel black stripes running the length of the body. Yellow bass have roughly the same pattern, but against a gold background.

White and yellow bass are fussy about habitat. Whites require very large lakes and reservoirs, with deep, clear water. They adapt well when stocked in new waters that meet their needs, but yellow bass, for unknown reasons, have done poorly outside their natural range.

BLACK, BROWN AND YELLOW BULLHEAD CATFISH

North American records: Black – 8lb; Lake Wabcabuc, New York, 1951. Brown – 5lb 8oz; Veal Pond, Georgia, 1975. Yellow – 4lb 4oz; Mormon Lake, Arizona, 1984.

■ **RANGE:** Eastern U.S. and Canada.

■ **HABITAT:** Variable; ponds, lakes, large streams and rivers, usually where current is slack.

■ **MAIN FOODS:** Invertebrates, fish, insects, carrion, some plant matter.

The scent of worms, minnows or a special catfish stinkbait, carried through the water in the tiniest of quantities, is enough to set the bullhead off on the hunt. Using its fine-honed sense of smell, it circles in on the source of the smell, until it zeros in on the bait.

OPPOSITE *Fooled by a lure meant for bigger fish, this white bass was taken on a spoon, fished deep with a downrigger. On light tackle, this panfish is fine game.*

ABOVE *The early morning sun gilds the mist as another fishing day begins.*

All three species of bullheads are bottom-feeders, cruising just above the lake bed with their barbels twitching. The barbels – "whiskers" to most fishermen – are delicate sensory organs that help the catfish navigate and feed in darkness or in turbid water. For protection, the bullhead has spines in its dorsal and pectoral fins, connected to glands that can secrete a mildly venomous liquid.

Color is of little help in telling one species of bullhead from another, and such differences are perhaps best left to the experts.

■ CHANNEL CATFISH ■

North American record: 58lb; Santee-Cooper Reservoir, South Carolina, 1964.

■ **RANGE:** Stocked widely.

■ **HABITAT:** Cool lakes and rivers.

■ **MAIN FOODS:** Fish, insects, crayfish, invertebrates.

Unlike the other, sluggish members of the catfish family, the channel cat is a vigorous fighter, especially those that live in rivers, contesting the current all their lives. They are slimmer than many catfish, with deeply forked tails, bluish color and scattered spots (the larger blue catfish is similar, but usually lacks the channel catfish's spots.) They regularly achieve weights of 20 pounds, although the average in most waters is probably 10 pounds or less.

Because it is such an active feeder, and inhabits areas with other game fish, channel cats are often caught on lures meant for other species. Many an angler has reared back on what he thought was a trophy smallmouth, only to find a big channel catfish has taken his plug.

■ CARP ■

North American record: 57lb 13oz; Tidal Basin, Washington, D.C., 1983.

■ **RANGE:** European native stocked widely.

■ **HABITAT:** Adaptable; from muddy stock ponds and clean lakes to rivers and brackish waters.

■ **MAIN FOODS:** Scavenges on bottom for plant and animal foods.

The carp, revered as a fine food fish in Europe, has been a disastrous addition to North America's waterways, even though it can provide good fishing action and (depending on the water) passable eating.

Carp are minnows, closely related to domestic goldfish. Their high, humped back, muddy gold color and down-turned mouth with two small barbels are diagnostic. They can grow quite large, and in most large lakes the average is usually between 10 and 15 pounds. The presence of carp has, unfortunately, degraded many previously high-quality waters. Grubbing for food on the lake bottom, they roil the mud, uprooting aquatic plants and destroying the eggs of native fish.

Still, carp have their good points. They are tenacious fighters, bull-dogging against the rod, and catching large carp on light tackle is akin to hooking a truck. From cool, clean water, carp fillets can be as tasty as most panfish, although the flesh does tend to be mushy from warm water, and picks up the less agreeable flavors from polluted waters.

OPPOSITE A European import with few redeeming values, the carp easily overpopulates lakes and rivers, degrading the water while providing some fishing enjoyment.

Chapter Four

PUTTING IT ALL TOGETHER

Trout fishing

■ GENERAL TACKLE AND TECHNIQUES ■

Speaking in broad generalities, trout are usually stream dwellers, and are normally under 15 inches, making them perfect candidates for ultralight fishing with either bait or lures. Tastes vary, but the ideal trout rig for stream fishing would be an ultralight spinning outfit loaded with 4-pound monofilament. A 5-foot rod (a little shorter than most) provides greater maneuverability in tight quarters than longer poles. For fly-fishing on streams, a 5- or 6-weight outfit, with an 8-foot-long rod, is hard to beat. By using floating line, you'll have the versatility to switch from dry flies to streamers without changing line, because in the fairly shallow waters of a stream, the leader provides enough depth to sink a wet fly to the bottom. In addition, floating line is easier to lift off the water, making casting much less frustrating.

■ DRIFTING BAIT ■

Like all fish, trout will fall for a well-fished natural bait. Worms and minnows top the list, but grasshoppers, crickets and hellgrammites work well, too.

Trout, especially those that have been fished over regularly, have a reputation for intelligence. When bait-fishing, therefore, try as much as possible to imitate the natural movement of unfettered food. Use as little weight as possible – just enough to get the bait down to the level where the trout are holding, but not enough to keep it from tumbling along in the current.

For worm fishing, a light hook, about size 6, works best. Thread the worm onto the hook so most of the shank is hidden and the worm can writhe as it normally would – do not make a ball or gob. When fishing nightcrawlers, the temptation often is to use too big a worm; it is better to pinch larger crawlers in half, so the trout is more likely to grab the portion that contains your hook. One or two small splitshot, a foot above the hook, are usually all the weight you'll need. Watch how the worm acts in the current, and adjust the amount of lead accordingly. If the worm drifts near the surface, add another splitshot, because trout will hang near the bottom, especially early in spring, when bait-fishing is most effective.

Minnows can be fished alive, hooked through the lips or tail, but most stream fishermen prefer freshly dead minnows. One very effective rig calls for a special "minnow needle," a large (3-inch) needle with one side of the eye cut away, and a double minnow hook. Tie a swivel onto your line, then attach an 18-inch section of mono to act as a leader. Tie a surgeon's loop at the end of the leader, then hook the needle in the loop. Using the needle, thread the loop down the mouth of a small, dead minnow and out of the anus. Slip the open shank of the double minnow hook over the loop and pull the loop – and with it the shank – into the body of the minnow. The two hook points should curve up and forward on each side of the bait. With one

OPPOSITE In the shade of wild rhododendrons, a fisherman tries his luck on a Pennsylvania mountain trout stream.

ABOVE Sea-run steelhead are tough adversaries, and call for substantial tackle on either spinning or fly-fishing gear.

ABOVE *For fly-fishing for stream trout like these stocked rainbows, a 5- or 6-weight outfit is best.*

or two splitshot for weight, fish the minnow across and slightly downstream, allowing it to swing through the current. As it moves, the minnow will spin – the reason for the swivel, so the line doesn't become hopelessly twisted.

ULTRALIGHT SPINNERS

Flashy spinners have long been regarded as top trout-getters, and with good reason. Even small trout take minnows, and as they grow larger, their dependence on forage fish increases. Spinners imitate small, fast-moving bait fish, and even offer some advantages over the real thing – ease of handling, for instance. In many situations, tiny spinners are deadly on trout of all sizes, but to effectively fish such bantam-weight lures, you must use light tackle.

Using an ultralight outfit and 2- or 4-pound line, tie on a small swivel, size 14 or 16. To it tie on a 1-foot length of mono leader the same size as the line; the swivel is simply to prevent line twist. Most spinner brands come in a range of sizes, down to ¹⁄₃₂ of an ounce. For ultralight work, those from ⅛ ounce and smaller work best.

Using the small spinner, keep your casts short, working pocket water, where rocks and logs provide eddies, or where tree roots overhang the water. The small lure makes little noise when it splashes down, so ultralight spinners are good choices, too, for flat, calm stretches where trout tend to be especially wary. Fish across stream and down, letting the current sweep the lure along. As a matter of

course, fish the spinner as slow as possible while still making the blade revolve. Start with steady retrieves, but if that doesn't produce, try imparting action to the spinner with twitches, jerks and short pauses. In very early spring, when the water is still cold, fish the spinner with excruciating slowness, even bumping it along the bottom. At such times trout tend to be sluggish, and won't bother to attack a lure going any faster.

▌ NIGHT FISHING FOR BIG TROUT ▌

As mentioned earlier, large trout often spend the day holed up in protective cover, only coming out after dark to gorge on minnows. Take advantage of that by fishing after sundown, using bait fish or minnow imitations.

Night fishing is equally effective on streams or lakes. Avoid using a flashlight any more than necessary as it may spook fish, and if you let your eyes adjust to the darkness, you'll be able to see well enough to cast. A small, flexible-neck pocket light, widely used by fly-fishermen, is perfect for tying knots and changing lures. Rely on your ears to tell you when the strike comes, and to locate trout splashing and feeding in the shallows.

Because night is the time for big fish, use strong tackle and big lures: a medium spinning outfit with 6- or 8-pound line, or a fly rig with a 6-pound tippet. Large spinners, minnow-shaped plugs like Rebels and Rapalas, large streamers and real minnows all work very well. Fish them slow with a lot of action, because night-hunting trout use their lateral line nerves to sense movement in the water. Surprisingly, black is usually the most reliable lure color, perhaps because it shows up well when silhouetted by the star-lit sky.

■ FISHING THE GRASSHOPPER "HATCH" ■

In late summer across much of North America, the land comes alive with grasshoppers, some of which, unavoidably, tumble into the water and the waiting jaws of hungry trout. Grasshoppers (and in some areas crickets) can provide some of the best trout fishing of the year.

Real grasshoppers make good bait, although they can be difficult to keep hooked. Fish them on the surface, if possible, and try to match with your casts the hopper's habit of falling to the water right at shoreside. To extend your casts, a clear plastic casting bubble works well.

Fly-fishing with grasshopper imitations can be even more productive than using live bait, because there is no fuss with collecting, storing or replacing real grasshoppers. There are a wealth of patterns modeled after grasshoppers – Joe's Hopper, Dave's Hopper, Elk-hair Hoppers and others. Sizes vary with the local species, but most have a clipped deer-hair head for buoyancy, a yellow or green body, a touch of red at the tail and a wing of trimmed turkey quill. For extra realism, some have large hind legs made of knotted feather shafts.

The heaviest grasshopper action is often at midday, when the sun has warmed the bugs into activity. Trout take up feeding stations right along the bank, usually where the current has cut a deep channel and the vegetation hangs over. Watch for the rise of a feeding trout, then drop the fly tight against the bank and just upstream. Another technique that sometimes works is to slap the fly down just *behind* the fish, which may react to the sound by turning and nailing the artificial.

Bass fishing

■ GENERAL TACKLE AND TECHNIQUES ■

There is nothing delicate about bass; when they strike it is usually with a smash, and they are bruisers on the line. That's why most bass fishermen use tackle with more backbone than is needed for trout. In most cases, medium spinning and bait-cast outfits with 6- or 8-pound line will do, but where the bass are big, or the cover thick, going to 12- or even 14-pound line isn't a bad idea.

Largemouths and smallmouths are both bass, but as previously noted, their habits and habitats differ widely. Generally speaking, imitations of minnows, frogs, worms and crayfish – plus their real counterparts, of course – are the most consistent producers.

■ PLASTIC WORMS FOR LARGEMOUTHS ■

Plastic, or "rubber," worms may be the best all-round lure for largemouth bass. For rigging instructions, see Chapter 1, *Getting Started*.

BELOW The biggest trout usually feed after dark, when they can hunt for minnows with impunity. Big streamers or plugs are the best nighttime lures.

OPPOSITE The lake surface erupts as a largemouth bass comes unwillingly to the boat, fighting all the way.

A plastic worm is a highly expressive lure, that is, even the tiniest twitch of the rod is telegraphed in its movements, making it a very versatile artificial. Work the worm on or near the bottom, bumping it along through weedbeds and over logs. In most cases, fishing the worm very slowly pays the biggest dividends, but don't hesitate to try varying the retrieve speed if that doesn't work. Plastic worms, especially those with curled or auger tails, work well as a mid-water lure, and can even be fished at or just below the surface. Jigging with a lightly weighted worm can also be effective, particularly if the fisherman is alert for soft strikes as the worm sinks on slack line. In fact, the only limit on how to fish a plastic worm is the angler's imagination – bass like them so much, they rarely fail.

CRAYFISH AND HELLGRAMMITES FOR SMALLMOUTHS

In many rivers, smallmouth bass eat little besides crayfish (sometimes known as crawdads,) making them a perfect choice as bait. Hell-grammites do not usually form the majority of a bass' diet, but are eagerly taken when the opportunity arises.

To work well, crayfish must be used live, which raises a problem as their natural urge is to dive for the rocks and hide. You can combat it in several ways. A small bobber several feet above the crayfish should keep it from reaching bottom, although it may interfere with strike detection (in fast water where currents conflict, the float will bounce constantly, making it tough to judge when a fish is on). Hook the crayfish through the tail, slipping the hook under one of the shell plates. Crayfish can also be hooked through the back, or attached to the hook with a rubber-band. Regardless, cast gently, because they rip from the hook easily.

Many smallmouth rivers are shallow enough to wade, so try fishing a live crawdad on a short line. Keep the rod tip high and don't let the line go slack, or the crayfish will dive for the bottom, where you will probably lose it. Work the bait through eddies at the head of pools, slicks near fast water, and around ledges and drop-offs, wading care-fully to avoid spooking the bass.

Hellgrammites are fished in much the same way, but because they don't swim well, they don't pose quite the problem that crayfish do. Use a small hook and slip it under the insect's collar, or thorax. A small amount of weight may be necessary to get the bait deep enough, but too much will only deaden its natural drift and reduce strikes.

FISHING WITH PLUGS

Plugs, both surface and diving models, are terrific for bass in almost any setting. Surface plugs generally work best early and late, when bass are feeding more actively, while deep-water plugs like crankbaits may produce at any time.

The most common mistake in fishing surface plugs is working them too fast. As a rule, drop the lure with a cast, then wait until the ripples have died away before moving it. The noise of the lure splashing down may startle nearby bass for a moment, but their curiosity will bring

OPPOSITE *A brown plastic worm, fished slowly through the lily pads, proved irresistible to this nice largemouth.*

BELOW *The variety of plastic worm shapes and colors is staggering, as is the range of worm hook styles that are available.*

ABOVE *A crayfish, just the right size for smallmouth bass, is rigged with a short-shank hook through the tail. Some anglers also peel off a section of tail shell to release more scent.*

them back for a closer look. The bass may strike the motionless lure, or it may wait for the first, tentative twitch. If there is no response, wait a moment, then slowly begin to retrieve the lure in spurts. Progress should be almost painfully slow, to imitate the feeble movements of an injured fish or frog. If the retrieve is too fast, the bass may simply follow the lure for a distance, then lose interest.

There are exceptions to every rule, of course, and on some days, a quick retrieve will draw strikes from bass that ignored slower-moving plugs. If one method doesn't work, don't become locked into a single pattern. Experiment, until you find out what the bass want.

The same goes for fishing diving and sinking plugs. A somewhat faster retrieve, with plenty of rod action, normally works best, but at times a stop-and-start approach, or a blisteringly fast return, pay off.

OPPOSITE A deer-hair or cork popper is one of the best lures for smallmouth bass, especially in late summer and fall.

ABOVE When fishing surface plugs, start slow, covering the water carefully, then switch to different retrieve speeds if you find the fish aren't hitting.

BIG FISH FOR BIG BASS

Southern fishermen know that to catch trophy largemouths, you need something to tempt their trophy-sized appetites. By using big shiners – six or eight inches long – you will reduce the number of fish you catch, but greatly increase your chances of a 10- or 12-pound bass. Hooked lightly through the lips, the shiners should be fished with a bobber but no weight, allowing it to swim near cover where a lunker may be hiding.

■ FLY-FISHING FOR BASS ■

Bass are one of the best quarries for the fly-fishermen because of their strength and wide distribution. Because the flies (and usually the fish) are bigger than in trout fishing, a heavier outfit is needed; for smallmouths, a 7- or 8-weight rod and reel is recommended, while large waters and big fish call for rods as heavy as 9-weight. Leaders should be appropriately heavy, with tippets of 6 to 10 pounds or more.

Bass flies come in a riot of shapes and colors. Topwater patterns include deer hair and cork poppers like the Sneaky Pete or Gerbubble Bug, deer hair diving bugs like the Dahlberg Diver series and deer hair mouse or frog imitations. Many of the fly-rod patterns echo spinning lures: crawler, marabou leech and waterpup flies have an action similar to plastic worms and jigs, while any number of large, flashy streamers will produce as well as minnow-shaped plugs. Others are strictly imitative, matching hellgrammites, crayfish and the larvae of dragonflies.

For pure excitement, it's hard to beat fly-rodding with surface bugs, both for smallmouths and largemouths. On lakes and ponds, use weedless bugs that have a loop of heavy monofilament tied at the hook bend and eye to deflect snags. Fish tight against cover, working the bug slowly through lily pads, brush and weedbeds. Fishing from shore, cast parallel to the bank and only a foot or two out from the edge, where bass will lurk for frogs and insects.

RIGHT Spinners, spoons and plugs all work well for northern pike, from small "hammer-handles" to 25-pound trophies.

BELOW In spring, pike can be found in shallow coves, dropping into deeper water as the summer progresses. They have an affinity for weedbeds, as well as brushpiles and other cover.

In rivers, surface bugs – especially poppers – take plenty of small-mouth, especially in late summer and fall when water levels are low and the fish are trying to fatten for the upcoming winter. Combinations of red, yellow and white seem to work particularly well, fished in eddies and riffles. The strike, when it comes, will be explosive, sending water flying through the air.

Pike and pickerel fishing

▋ GENERAL TACKLE AND TECHNIQUES ▋

The only substantive difference between pike and pickerel is size. Both feed with the same, methodical stalk, attack with the same gutsy rush and fight with the same spirit. Both have lean bodies and tooth-studded mouths. But while pickerel are hard pressed to reach 4 pounds, pike can grow to 10 times that size.

Fishing techniques for pike and pickerel, therefore, are similar in everything except degree. For pickerel, light- or medium-weight spinning tackle works fine, although a foot-long shock leader of heavy monofilament or hard nylon is a good idea to guard against those sharp teeth. For pike, most anglers prefer medium or heavy gear, depending on the size of the pike expected; a 25-pounder will test your rod and reel to the limits. A steel leader will prevent slash-offs, although a heavy monofilament leader will usually provide adequate protection, without the lure-sinking weight of steel.

Virtually any lure may work for pike and pickerel, because they are notoriously unselective in their feeding habits. Diving, minnow-shaped plugs are consistent producers, as are spinners, spoons, flies and jigs. Fish weedbeds and structure, especially overgrown banks, brushpiles and sunken logs.

▌ SPOONS – THE OLD STANDBY ▌

No lure has produced as many pike over the years as the simple spoon, or wobbler. In parts of Canada and the Great Lakes states, where trophy pike are the quarry, other lures have traditionally been dismissed with a contemptuous wave of the hand.

Spoon colors range through the spectrum, but if you want to play the odds, tie on a red-and-white, the combination that has probably accounted for more pike through the years than any other. Silver, silver-and-blue, chartreuse and orange are also good at times.

BELOW Spoons can be fished by casting, trolling or vertical jigging near promising cover. This silver-and-blue spoon accounted for a good stringer of Canadian northern pike.

ABOVE To interest a muskellunge's fickle temperament, lures must be large; flash and color seem to help in making the catch, although drab lures sometimes work well, too.

OPPOSITE Pike can provide unmatched sport on fly tackle, slamming streamers and poppers with gusto and battling both above and below the surface.

There are several ways to fish spoons. By drifting near likely pike cover and casting, you can cover a large amount of water. In a steady retrieve, the spoon will oscillate from side to side with a seductive wobble. By changing direction in mid-retrieve, and by adding some twitches and tugs from the rod, the spoon becomes even more inviting to the pike. Even a dead stop can bring strikes, as the spoon flutters straight down.

Trolling spoons can be very good for pike, especially if they are holding offshore on deep structure. Try varying the trolling speed and depth until you find the one that the pike want.

In lakes with deep drop-offs and lots of brush, vertical jigging can be a killer. Ease the boat right up to the brushpile and drop the spoon over the side, jigging it up and down. If there is pike lurking within the branches, it may hesitate for a moment, but the sight of the spoon dancing and flashing under its nose will eventually prod it into a

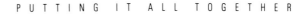

slamming strike. For this kind of fishing you'll need somewhat heavier line and gear, because the pike must be immediately pulled out of the brushpile before it can wrap the line around a branch and break off.

■ FLY-FISHING FOR PIKE AND PICKEREL ■

Both pike and pickerel are great fun on a fly rod. A standard trout or bass outfit will serve fine for pickerel, but big pike call for a brawny 9- or 10-weight set, loaded with floating line, a heavy, braided leader and a tippet of 20-pound-test hard nylon, which resists the pike's teeth better than monofilament.

Many bass bugs work well for pike and pickerel, especially those that imitate frogs and mice. Flashy streamers are good as well – 1 or 2 inches long for pickerel, up to 8 inches in length for pike. Streamers tied with prismatic tinsel, such as the Flashabou brand, are super pike getters. Generally speaking, bright colors work best in spring, and darker tones later in the summer.

■ BAIT-FISHING ■

Fishing live bait may be the single most productive way to catch pike and pickerel. Minnows, shiners and small perch are the baits of choice. Hook the fish lightly through the lips, under the dorsal fin or just ahead of the tail, then clip on a bobber several feet above it. The minnow should be allowed to swim freely, and must be replaced if it dies – movement alone will attract the pike. The bobber usually provides the first hint that a strike is coming, as the panicked minnow makes a last dash to escape, towing the float along behind.

The strike will probably be sudden, but resist the temptation to set the hook immediately. Pickerel and pike both feed by grabbing their prey, running a short distance with it, then repositioning the minnow to gulp it down. Wait through the first short run with an open reel ball, so the line plays out freely. When the fish stops, wait a moment, then drive the hook home. A powerful hook set is called for, because pike, in particular, have bony mouths. The list of other live baits is long – frogs, salamanders, even live mice, although using a mammal for bait is more than most fishermen can stand to do.

Walleye fishing

■ GENERAL TACKLE AND TECHNIQUES ■

Except in the rarest of circumstances, catching walleyes means fishing deep. These tasty school fish hug the bottom, only coming into the shallows at night, or on heavily overcast days.

Walleyes can get big, up to 9 or 10 pounds, but most of those caught are in the 1- to 3-pound range, making them perfect for light or medium tackle. Fishing light for walleyes also has the benefit of accentuating the fight, which is markedly listless in most individuals. Walleyes are terrific eating fish, but on a line they are usually lackluster. For larger walleye, a heavy leader is a good idea, because their teeth,

while not as large as a pike's, are every bit as tough on monofilament.

When fishing for walleyes, an electronic depthfinder or fishfinder is invaluable for spotting underwater structure like drop-offs where the schools congregate. If you don't have a depthfinder, a discerning eye for the contours of the surrounding land (which may be echoed underwater) and some trolling should put you into a school. Early in the morning, make a point of searching out deep water that is shaded from the sun, where walleyes may still be feeding actively.

Bait accounts for plenty of walleye each year, as do jigs, spinners, spoons and diving, minnow-shaped plugs.

Night fishing is perhaps the most productive method of walleye fishing, especially for trophy fish. On most waters the best times are from midnight to 3 a.m., although a bright moon or cloudy water may alter that timetable.

▮ BAIT-FISHING FOR WALLEYES ▮

Fish make up the bulk of a walleye's diet, so it's no surprise that minnows, alive or dead, are a proven bait.

Where the water is shallow enough, fish an unweighted live minnow below a bobber. For greater depth, a slip sinker, or one of the newer "walking sinkers" that prevent snags, are needed to take the bait down to the walleye. The strike will usually be soft, a delicate tapping rather than a sudden jerk, but your response must be firmer, because a walleye has a hard, toothy mouth.

Worms and leeches are also excellent walleye baits, either fished on a bare hook or as dressing for a jig or spinner. Leeches have the advantage of being almost indestructible, but can be harder to get in some areas.

RIGHT Walleye are primarily *fish-eaters, so a minnow – fished live or rigged dead with a spinner – is a highly effective bait.*

LEFT A white jig added this Quebec walleye to the stringer.

▌ JIGS AND SPINNERS ▌

Among artificial lures, jigs and spinners are tops for walleye, especially if they are combined with bait – the standard procedure in most regions.

The most popular jig colors are white, yellow and green; red, orange, black and pink can work well also. While standard lead-headed jigs remain popular, more and more fishermen are switching to floating jig heads, used with a sinker rigged to a dropper line a foot or two ahead of the lure. With such a rig, the sinker takes the line deep, but the floating jig head keeps the lure just off the bottom. As an added benefit, the dropper line can be tied of lighter monofilament than the main line, so if the sinker snags it can be broken free, saving the more expensive lure.

Jigs can be fished vertically over the side of the boat, by casting or trolling. A minnow, fish strip, leech or worm dangling from the hook will greatly increase your catch; apparently the color and twisting jig tail attracts the walleye's attention, but the smell of the bait makes them strike.

Snelled spinners are a walleye-fishing specialty. One or more hooks are snelled to a heavy mono leader, with colored beads and a metal or painted spinner blade in front. The bait is strung on the hooks so it streams out behind the spinners, which – as with jigs – catch the walleye's notice. Snelled spinners can be purchased unweighted or as floating rigs, which prevent snags. Combinations of red, yellow, green and white, usually fluorescents, work best.

ABOVE Most panfish fly-rod poppers have long rubber legs, which wiggle at the slightest twitch and drive the fish crazy.

RIGHT Catching bluegills and other sunfish is an uncomplicated affair, whether on bait or artificials.

Panfish fishing

■ GENERAL TACKLE AND TECHNIQUES ■

It's hard to generalize about panfish, because the group includes such a variety of fish – bullheads, sunfish, carp, crappies and more – each requiring somewhat different tackle. Bluegills, crappies, perch and white and yellow bass are best enjoyed on ultralight tackle or light-weight fly rods, while big carp will strain even heavy gear.

■ CANEPOLE BLUEGILLS – AN OUTDOOR CLASSIC ■

Who said fishing has to be complicated? Take a long bamboo canepole or a limber greenwood switch, tie on a 10-foot length of monofilament and a hook, and you're ready to catch bluegills and other sunfish in the time-honored way. A gob of worms for bait and a tiny, red-and-white bobber complete the picture.

Once, a stack of canepoles was found in every tackle shop, but today, unfortunately, they can be hard to find. For those who want a higher-tech version, there are telescoping fiberglass panfish rods, in lengths up to 20 feet, with a small reel built into the handle. Fiberglass or bamboo, the technique is the same; drift in a boat or fish from a dock, with the bobber set a few feet above the bait to keep the worms suspended. Usually before the ring has disappeared after the cast, the bobber will begin dancing as small sunfish nibble at the hook. The bobber may even plunge for a moment as a fingerling takes a running grab at a worm. Wait, though, for the bobber to dive deep before setting the hook – you are more likely to latch onto an eating-sized bluegill that way.

▌ ULTRALIGHT CRAPPIES ▌

In spring, not too many weeks after ice-out, the crappie swarm into the shallows to breed. At such times action can be fantastic and because panfish usually overpopulate a lake, taking breeding fish will probably have no serious impact on the crappie fishery.

Crappie are minnow eaters, so tiny plugs and jigs are the top lures, but to use them to their fullest advantage, one must fish with light gear. Ultralight spinning rods, small reels and 2- or 4-pound test mono are just about right.

Plastic jigs account for many of the crappies taken, but lots of fishermen still prefer old-fashioned marabou jigs, with plastic or chenille bodies. The jigs can be fished vertically into brushpiles, or by casting; with open-face spinning gear, try sticking your index finger

BELOW *Light and ultralight tackle bring out the best in a crappie, transmitting every surge and lunge in the fight.*

LEFT *Rock bass – one of the dozens of panfish species found across North America – are small but scrappy fighters.*

down into the returning line, so it slaps against the finger. The result is a rapid pulse that travels down the line and makes the marabou flick with a motion that crappies seem to love.

On windy days, jigs can also be fished with a bobber. Set the float high enough above the jig so the lure will be down at the crappies' level, then cast. The waves will bounce the bobber – and the jig – imitating the natural movement of bait fish.

▌ BAIT-FISHING FOR CATFISH ▌

Fishing for bullheads and other catfish is a sedentary sport, a waiting game played out on lawn chairs, with rods braced on forked sticks jammed in the mud.

Almost any sort of bait will work for catfish, but the smellier, normally, the better. Some catfish anglers swear by stinkbaits, while others prefer fresh red meat, fish strips, cheese, liver, chicken skin or entrails, worms, minnows or doughballs. All agree, however, that the bait's aroma is the draw, pulling in catfish from long distances.

Because catfish are bottom feeders, use enough lead to sink the bait to the bottom and keep it there; a moving bait will only reduce the catfish's chances of making the connection. Most fishermen cast, wait for the bait to settle to the bottom, then reel any slack out of the line. By bracing the rod with the tip high, the slightest nibble will be transmitted to the surface. Gently pick up the rod, and when you're sure the catfish has the bait, strike. Because the bait is usually swallowed, don't plan on releasing what you catch – the fish is often badly injured, and should be taken home to eat.

▌ FISHING FOR CARP ▌

Carp may lack the glamour of a pike or trout, but fishing for them can be exciting, especially if the carp is a giant of 20 or 30 pounds. Don't expect jumping and other surface antics – the effect is similar to hooking a submarine.

Like catfish, carp are bottom feeders that rely on smell to lead them to food. Worms and corn kernels are proven baits, but serious carp fishermen prefer doughballs, made of cornmeal, flour and water, then flavored with just about anything aromatic. Fruit-flavored gelatins work well, as does vanilla extract, oil of anise, almond flavoring or honey. The dough is molded on the hook before each cast.

Your tackle must be substantial when fishing for carp, with a good drag on the reel. Carp are not difficult to fool, so go with fairly heavy line – 10 or 15 pounds. Terminal tackle should include hooks in sizes 6 or 4, and enough weight to get the bait to the bottom.

For a challenge, try carp on lighter gear. They can even be taken on fly rods, using a small weighted nymph. In the spring, when carp spawn, hundreds can occasionally be found in the shallows of streams and rivers. Cast the fly just upstream from the fish and allow it to swing across the current in front of their noses. The fight will lack the grace of a leaping trout, but as the rod bucks and the line screams off the reel, you won't really care.

OPPOSITE A carp isn't glamorous, but it fights with bulldog tenacity and great strength.

RIGHT *Bundled against the cold dawn, a family heads out for a day of fishing.*

After the catch

▌ CLEANING AND STORING FISH ▌

Preferences vary, but almost all game fish – properly cleaned and stored – are good eating. The important word here is "properly;" keeping a stringer of trout in the bottom of the boat all day, or carrying a bass in an unrefrigerated plastic bag on the three-hour drive home, is not the way to get the most from their natural flavor.

Correct handling begins before you've made your first cast. If you intend to keep a few fish for a meal, plan ahead. Make sure you have a live well or stringer, and an ice chest in which to carry the catch home.

By far the best alternative is to keep the fish alive as long as possible. An aerated live well is unmatched, but isn't practical unless you're fishing in a large, fairly expensive boat. A stringer or a collapsible wire fish basket are more reasonable alternatives. With a stringer, clip the fish through the lower lip – not through the gills, and not through the upper and lower jaw, which will suffocate it quickly. With a stringer or basket, be sure to pull the fish into the boat before moving to a new location, because the rapid flow can kill the fish – not to mention tear your catch loose from the stringer.

If you have an ice chest handy, the most humane alternative is to kill the fish immediately with a quick, sharp blow to the head, then ice it down. Not only is this the least cruel method, but it also produces the freshest flavor and best eating.

Many trout fishermen still swear by creels, either wicker or rubberized canvas. The secret to using a creel is to keep the fish inside as cool and moist as possible. Lining the creel with wet ferns, then keeping it in the shade, is the most effective procedure. Always kill the trout before creeling it; to allow it simply to flop to death, drowning in unbreathable air, is unspeakably cruel.

▌**FILLETING A FISH** Most fish are best filleted for cooking. Except for shad and members of the pike family, filleting produces two boneless portions of meat, and wastes very little of the usable parts of the fish.

Use a knife with a thin, narrow blade, whetted to a razor edge. Do not gut the fish; the entrails will simply be thrown away with the skeleton, still in the abdominal cavity.

▌**GUTTING A FISH** Trout under 15 inches can be cooked whole, without filleting. To clean them for the freezer, simply gut them, removing the entrails and gills.

▌ GEAR MAINTENANCE ▌

Modern fishing tackle is far more corrosion-resistant than that of the past. Still, rods, reels and other tackle requires some basic care to keep it in good shape from season to season.

The quality of monofilament line degrades with time and exposure to sunlight, weakening it. Most serious fishermen replace their line several times a season, although the average angler can easily get away with just an annual change.

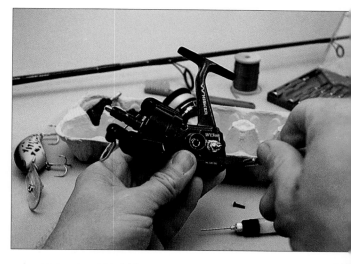

BELOW *To keep them in top condition, reels should be regularly stripped down, cleaned of grit and relubricated.*

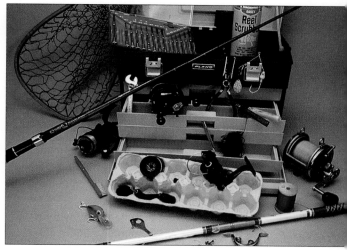

ABOVE *After the fishing season has ended for the winter, take time to organize tackle boxes, repair damaged gear and put things right for the next year.*

Carefully clean away any grit or sand that gets into your reel, especially under the line spool, and regrease everything with one of the reel lubricants on the market. Check periodically to make sure the bail hasn't been nicked – a seemingly minor accident that can slice your line during a fight.

Likewise, check the line guides on your rod for any rough spots or ragged edges, which can saw away at the line, parting it at a critical moment. A good method is to run a dry cotton swab around the inside of the guide – any roughness will pull cotton fibers loose. A nicked guide should be discarded; most large tackle supply companies stock replacements.

When storing rods for any length of time, avoid leaning them against a wall or in a corner. Over long periods, the rod may "memorize" the curve it picks up from leaning, thus ruining it. A much better idea is to store you rods either in metal or plastic rod cases, or vertically on a special wall-mounted rack.

After the last fishing trip of the year, take time to sort through your tackle boxes, cleaning out dirt and sand and reorganizing your lures. Check each lure for broken hooks, loose trebles or hooks with bent points. Use a hook sharpener on all your lures – not a bad idea throughout the season, either.

▌ CONSERVATION ▌

The fundamental idea behind fishing is to have fun. Such simple enjoyment can come as easily from successfully luring a scrappy blue-gill as from a monster pike. Yet there would be no enjoyment without fish, which is why every fisherman has a responsibility to be a good conservationist, as well.

That means not killing fish just so you can show off a big stringer, but taking only what you will eat. It means being gentle and careful with any fish you plan to return to the water. It also means being meticulous in your habits in the outdoors – in not littering (which includes unwanted monofilament fishing line, a notorious killer of birds and aquatic life,) and in not polluting the water with engine oil or gasoline.

Being a conservationist also means taking the larger view. There can be no fishing without clean water, so become a voice that demands strong pollution control laws and their strict enforcement. Join the fight against acid precipitation, which threatens so many of North America's lakes and streams. Speak out in favor of greenbelts to protect the watersheds of rivers and streams; against unnecessary water projects that will drown free-flowing rivers. Multiply your clout by joining an organization that seeks to preserve the environment on a national scale, but keep a close eye on developments close to home. If a private or governmental plan will damage local waterways, let yourself be heard, because the sign of a good fishermen isn't the size of the catch, but the care he or she takes with the environment that provides the fish in the first place.

OPPOSITE *Fishing waters are located in often beautiful and sometimes isolated locations, and it is the responsibility of the fisherman to contribute to their preservation and that of the environment.*

INDEX

Figures in *italics* refer to captions.

ACKNOWLEDGMENTS

Key: *t* = top; *b* = bottom; *l* = left; *r* = right; *c* = center.

© C. Boyd Pfeiffer: pages 8/9, 15 *t c*, 16 *l*, 18 *b*, 22 *t*, 26 *t*, 39, 40, 47 *t b*, 49, 51, 58, 60, 63, 67, 69, 71, 72, 74, 75, 76, 77 *t*, 78, 80 *b*, 83 *b*, 87 *t b*, 89, 91 *t b*, 92/3. © Chris Dawn: page 28. © Bernard "Lefty" Dreh: pages 32–33, 34–5 *t*. © Arthur Oglesby: page 48. © Outdoor Images/Randy Carrels: pages 7, 17 *l*, 26 *b*, 84. © Outdoor Images/Tom Huggler: pages 10, 11, 12/13, 14, 15 *b*, 16/17, 18 *t*, 24/5, 25 *r*, 27 *tr b*, 31, 35 *b*, 36 *t b*, 37, 38, 41, 43 *t*, 44, 45, 46, 53, 54, 55, 56, 57, 59 *t b*, 61, 62, 64/65, 66, 80 *t*, 82/3, 86 *r*, 90. © Joe Reynolds: pages 6, 19 *b*, 27 *t l*, 42, 43 *b*, 52, 79. © Marcus Schneck: pages 17 *r*, 19 *t*, 20, 21, 23 *t*, 70, 77 *b*, 81, 85, 86 *l*. © Scott Weidensaul: pages 22 *b*, 23 *b*, 73.